THE GROWTH OF THE SPANISH INQUISITION

Ximenes is praised by many who declare him worthy of sainthood. But reflect for a moment on an account of the numbers of his victims: 3,564 burnt at the stake; 1,232 burnt in effigy; and penitents who suffered from confiscation of worldly goods and other punishments, 48,059 ...

Fifty-two thousand people is a large number; one can be sure that every one of these would be very doubtful of the claim of Ximenes' admirers that the latter was a saint.

What can we really know of this man? Not a great deal. We can though be sure of this: under his guidance the Inquisition firmly planted by Torquemada became that sturdy growth which was so firmly rooted in Spanish soil that it was able to exist through the seventeenth and eighteenth centuries and into the nineteenth.

Also by Jean Plaidy in *Star*:
MARY QUEEN OF SCOTS: THE FAIR DEVIL OF SCOTLAND
THE RISE OF THE SPANISH INQUISITION

To be published shortly:
THE END OF THE SPANISH INQUISITION

THE GROWTH
OF THE
SPANISH INQUISITION

Jean Plaidy

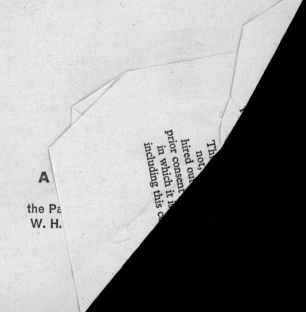

A

the Pa
W. H.

A Star Book
Published in 1978
by the Paperback Division of
W. H. Allen & Co. Ltd
A Howard and Wyndham Company
44 Hill Street, London W1X 8LB

First published in Great Britain by
Robert Hale Ltd, 1960

Printed in Great Britain by
Cox & Wyman Ltd,
London, Reading and Fakenham

ISBN 0 352 30216 X

NOTE
In order to avoid footnotes, sources and references are given
in the text.
My very special thanks are due to the librarians of
Kensington Public Library who have worked so hard and
patiently to procure rare books for me, and thus have aided
me considerably in my research.

CONTENTS

INTRODUCTION

United Spain was born in that fateful year of 1492 – and it seemed that about its cradle were gathered all the gifts the good fairies had to offer. Its governors were those two sovereigns–Ferdinand the soldier, Isabella the administrator – both monarchs in their own right and each endowed with qualities which, even had they reigned alone, would have brought greatness to Spain.

After seven hundred years of Moorish occupation, Spain (under Isabella and Ferdinand) had driven the enemy from the land. Over the Alhambra in the last Moorish town to hold out, now flew the standard of Christian Spain.

The gifts the good fairies had to offer were glittering indeed; and perhaps the significance of the greatest of these gifts was not realized when it was handed to the sovereigns. This was the gift of a new world, which – as that of Christian Spain – must depend for its value on the use to which it was put.

Christian Spain had long been the dream of the sovereigns; this they had planned for, worked and fought for. The development of their country, from a bickering group of states with a Mussulman enemy within their midst to a united land, must have seemed little short of miraculous. When they had married in 1469, Isabella's brother Henry IV had been alive, and his daughter (had she not been almost certainly illegitimate) would have been heir to the throne of Castile. But the war of succession had been won, the Treaty of Lisbon signed in 1479 and Isabella had become Queen of Castile while Ferdinand, on the death of his father in 1479, had inherited the throne of Aragon. In twelve years the sovereigns had replaced with justice and order the anarchical rule of Isabella's father John II and her brother Henry IV; this in itself would have brought great credit to them if they had not won the additional merit of completing the reconquest. It was a record of which they could be justifiably proud.

From small states they had made one great country which had every opportunity of becoming the leading country of the world. And as if this were not enough, seemingly limitless possibilities had been laid at their feet, for on the 12th October of this glorious year a navigator who had set out on a voyage of discovery under the aegis of Isabella came upon a new land.

So far the Portuguese had been leading in nautical adventures. The Infante Henry (known as Henry the Navigator), who was the son of John I of Portugal, had already discovered the Madeira Islands and had explored the coast of Africa as far as Cape Blanco. (As his mother was a daughter of John of Gaunt one wonders whether his great love of and talent for exploration came from English forbears.) Henry also has the distinction of being the first to use a compass in navigation.

The Spaniards, however, were not far behind their neighbours on the high seas. They had taken possession of the Canary Islands (the Fortunate Isles); and Ferdinand and Isabella were certainly fully aware of the wealth which could come from an Empire. Certain rivalry had already sprung up between Spain and Portugal, but these differences had been settled by the Treaty of Lisbon.

There were men who dreamed of great discoveries, and among these there appeared a Genoese named Christopher Columbus.

He was of humble origin, the son, it is said, of a weaver; but he had great dreams. He had studied mathematics at Pavia, but when he was fourteen, experiencing the call of the sea, he left Pavia to follow the life of adventure.

He continued to sail the seas until 1470 when he was in his twenties. (It is not certain in what year he was born. Most authorities give the date as 1446, but Bernaldez says that when he died in 1506 he was seventy – 'more or less'.) He then decided to go to Portugal. In that country congregated the adventurous men of the world, for the Portuguese government more than any other was inclined to listen to their plans for the discovery of new land and, what was more to the point, provide ships and crews for the journey.

Columbus firmly believed that there was land beyond the Atlantic, and it was his intention to state this belief to the King of Portugal, John II, and enlist his help.

But there were numerous adventurers in Lisbon all seeking to impress the King with their plans, and Columbus found obstruction wherever he turned; he therefore decided to leave Portugal for Spain in the hope that he would win more sympathy from the Spanish sovereigns. Thus Portugal lost the honour of sending the expedition which resulted in the most important of all land discoveries.

However, Columbus met with frustration in Spain. He had arrived at an inopportune period, for the sovereigns were deeply concerned with the great war against the Infidel, and it is easily understood that, being thus occupied, they had little time or money to spare for what might prove to be the dream of a visionary. But Columbus discovered a friend in Fray Juan Perez de Marchena who was guardian of the Andalusian convent of La Rabida; Fray Juan was very interested in Columbus's plans, and so eloquently did the latter talk of these that Fray Juan decided to put the adventurer in touch with a man who had great influence with the Queen because he had become her confessor: Fernando de Talavera.

This was unfortunate, for Talavera was the last man to help in such an enterprise. Deeply religious, intensely bigoted, he distrusted everything that was new; he was eager to complete the conquest of the Moors and it seemed the utmost folly, in his view, to dissipate money and energy on wild schemes of exploration. He put the matter before the sovereigns – from his own angle; and as a result the Council of Salamanca, which was set up to consider it, decided that the project was 'impracticable'; so Columbus, frustrated once more and feeling that he had wasted a great deal of time, prepared to leave Spain for France where he hoped for a more sympathetic hearing.

Before he left the country he paid a farewell visit to Fray Juan Perez de Marchena at the Convent of La Rabida, and there he found that Fray Juan was as disappointed as he was himself. But Fray Juan would not give up, and decided to make the journey to the Queen himself, even though she was at Santa Fé, the great camp which had been built before Granada.

As a result of this Columbus was asked to visit the Queen who would reimburse the expenses of his journey. He arrived at an important moment: Granada had capitulated.

He told the Queen that he was confident of reaching a hitherto undiscovered land. He stressed the riches of the East, which he believed he could reach by sailing westward across the Atlantic Ocean; and he did not forget to remind Isabella that, if new lands were discovered and brought under the domination of the sovereigns, they would be won for Holy Church and the Christian Faith.

The thought of great riches deeply attracted Ferdinand, and the hope of bringing pagans into the Church attracted Isabella. Ferdinand, however, was wary and inclined to listen to the arguments of Talavera. This was one of those occasions, however, when Isabella showed herself ready to act on her own responsibility. She declared that she would give Columbus what he asked, even if it were necessary to pawn her jewels to find the money.

So on the 3rd August, 1492, Columbus set sail for the unknown; on 12th October, after two months of danger on the high seas, land was sighted. America was discovered. Thus was a new world presented to newly-born united Spain.

But they were not all *good* fairies at the christening.

In March the edict expelling the Jews had been signed, and this new Spain was to be robbed of a hard-working section of the population, remarkable in their peculiar genius for creating financial prosperity wherever they lived. Here was one of the curses on the new-born infant, and one which was to have far-reaching repercussions.

And over the cradle there also loomed intolerance and bigotry; no person, high or low throughout the land, could feel completely free from fear.

The Inquisition was firmly established in Spain and showing signs of growing stronger. It threw a dark grim shadow over all the blessings which the good fairies were showering on newly-united Christian Spain.

CHAPTER ONE

THE END OF TORQUEMADA

The expulsion of the Jews was the highlight of Torquemada's career. From the time he had risen to power he had worked for this, and when he saw that pitiable army of refugees leaving the country which had been their home for centuries, wretchedly seeking new homes in unknown lands where they could not know what their reception would be, he must have felt that his life's work was accomplished. Spain was still not completely Christian for, as a price for the surrender of Granada, Boabdil, the last Moorish king, had asked that the Inquisition should not be set up in Granada and that the Moors living there (although subjects of Ferdinand and Isabella) should be allowed to follow their own religion; their request had been granted. And although Torquemada may have been dismayed at this leniency towards non-Christians, he was too old to begin a new campaign. He had expelled most of the Jews and only those who had been baptized were allowed to remain. The Moors must be left to his successors to deal with.

Another important event had occurred in that fateful year of 1492 which was to affect Torquemada although it happened outside Spain. Innocent VIII had died and during August a Conclave was held in Rome. There were great rivalries for the Papal throne and, after certain acts of bribery and simony on the part of wily Roderigo Borgia, he was elected Pope Alexander VI.

Alexander was a man of tremendous energy and it may have been that he was not pleased by the immense power the Inquisition was wielding in Spain for, in the hands of Torquemada, it had freed itself from the influence of Rome.

Moreover, many of the persecuted were wealthy people, and

their friends and relations, although they dared not raise their voices at home against the Inquisition (for to do so would immediately bring them into its power), sent out complaints in other directions; and to whom could these complaints be more advantageously addressed than to Pope Alexander who was already showing his disapproval of Torquemada?

As for Torquemada, he was widely increasing the powers of the Inquisition, so that the civil courts were actually coming under the jurisdiction of the Holy Office. Any magistrate who did not conform with Torquemada's wishes was judged tainted with heresy and forced to perform certain minor – but public – penances.

Alexander had already issued a decree directed against Torquemada, in which he stated that the Inquisition had no right to proceed against priests unless they first obtained the sanction of the Pope.

Torquemada, under the protection of his doting sovereigns, was ready to flout the Pope if need be; but he was making many enemies, not only among the magistrates but among the prelates.

In the Vatican, Alexander was alert. Pleasure-loving, seemingly lenient as he was, he was yet not the man to allow any to flout him with impunity and escape.

Torquemada had brought about the exodus of the Jews, but that did not mean he had abandoned his persecutions of these unfortunate people. Although it is very probable that he himself had Jewish blood (through his paternal grandmother) he continued suspicious of others who had it.

One of these was Juan Arias Davila, who was Bishop of Segovia. The Bishop's grandfather had been a Jew, and although his grandson had risen in the Church to such high rank, Torquemada set his inquisitors to pry into the past of his long-dead grandfather, although Juan Arias Davila at this time was himself an old man.

By dint of the usual examination and terrorizing of witnesses it was 'discovered' that the grandfather of the Bishop of Segovia had been guilty of celebrating the rites of his old religion although he had been baptized into the Christian Faith.

Now the usual action should be taken: The bones of the dead man dug up, put into the *sanbenito*, taken to the *quemadero* and publicly burned. That was not all; his family could not expect to continue in prosperity. Their lands and goods would be confiscated and they themselves robbed of their offices.

Davila was aware of the slight tension between Torquemada and Alexander, and he therefore wisely appealed to Alexander.

Alexander's response was to remind Torquemada that when prelates were to be charged with sins against the Church the matter must be undertaken by an Apostolic Court.

Davila then set out for Rome where he was received with great kindness by the Pope; his case was put before a court called together by Alexander, the charge was found to be false, and Alexander gave the Bishop a post in the retinue of his nephew, Cardinal Borgia of Monreale, who was about to set out for Naples to attend the coronation of Alfonso II.

This was a snub for Torquemada; but he brought forward charges against another Bishop, and in this case he was more successful. This victim was Pedro de Aranda, Bishop of Cala- horra. The case against him was that his father, a New Chris- tian, had committed the sin of turning back to the Law of Moses. Aranda, like Davila, went to Rome and was received there with that gracious charm which was an essential part of Alexander's personality. He was found innocent at the court set up by Alexander, and favours were showered upon him – no doubt as a further snub to Torquemada.

But Torquemada was a man of great power and he would not meekly suffer two such defeats. A further charge of personal Judaizing was brought against Aranda, and this time there were witnesses to bring forward evidence against him, so that the Pontifical Court could not fail to find him guilty. As a result, he was denuded of his benefices and imprisoned in Sant' Angelo. He died there after a few years' incarceration.

But these two bishops, during their sojourns in Rome, had carried many complaints against Torquemada to Alexander, and the Pope made up his mind that Torquemada should not much longer hold the post of Grand Inquisitor in Spain.

It was typical of Alexander that, while he planned to rob Torquemada of his office, he should maintain an illusion of great friendliness towards him. He decided to play upon the most obvious reason for the resignation of the Inquisitor-General.

Torquemada was an old man, he said (Alexander was sixty, but he looked upon himself as a superman), and the great tasks which the Inquisitor-General took upon himself were too much for him. Greatly did Alexander cherish Tomás de Torquemada who had laboured long for the glory of the Faith, but he had decided to appoint four helpers who would take over some of his more irksome duties, and thus, now that he had greater need of rest, he would be able to enjoy it.

Alexander, wily as ever, did not intend those whom he had chosen for the new appointments to be in any way inferior to Torquemada; their power should equal his; to have referred to them as 'assistants' was merely an example of that diplomatic tact which had sustained Alexander through his dangerous career.

Two of the four 'assistants' appointed by Alexander (Martin Ponce de Leon, Archbishop of Messina, and Don Francisco Sanchez de la Fuente, Bishop of Avila) assumed office with Torquemada, so that instead of there being one supreme head of the Inquisition there were now three in command; moreover, Alexander forthwith addressed all communications concerning the Inquisition to the Bishop of Avila.

This was a great blow to Torquemada's pride, and there can be no doubt that, had he been in better health, he would have bitterly opposed interference from Rome. But although Alexander had succeeded in reducing Torquemada's title of Inquisitor-General to one of mere courtesy, he was far from the scene of Torquemada's activities and did not realize the extent of the power which the Prior of the Holy Cross held over the sovereigns and the people of Spain.

Torquemada had made the Inquisition what it was; he was so much a part of it that no interference from outside – however powerful – could dislodge him.

The new Inquisitors, confident of their power, made a new

rule that they themselves should control the disposal of goods which had been confiscated from heretics instead of, as hitherto, turning it over to the treasury.

This ruling naturally incurred the immediate wrath of Ferdinand, whose chief interest in the Inquisition was the riches it poured into his ever hungry coffers.

He at once appealed to Alexander, and Alexander, eager to keep peace with the Spanish sovereigns, immediately gave orders to the Inquisitors to desist from the new practices.

Torquemada had another and more formidable adversary than Alexander. In 1496 he was so feeble in health that he could no longer remain at Court. One of his chief ailments was the gout (generally supposed to be the result of rich living, so that it seemed an odd quirk of fate that this ascetic man should be so afflicted) and he retired to the monastery he had built at Avila.

In spite of the fact that he was absent from Court he was not forgotten by Isabella who always held him in great affection and respect, and she and Ferdinand visited him at the monastery, which left no doubt in the minds of all that he stood as high in favour as he had ever done, and that the Pope's sly efforts to oust him had not been entirely successful.

During the last year of Torquemada's life the sovereigns suffered a great tragedy. Isabella loved all her children dearly, but the only son was naturally of especial importance to his parents. This was the Infante Juan who at eighteen years of age had been married to the Princess Margaret, the daughter of the Emperor Maximilian; and it was arranged that Margaret's brother (Archduke Philip, son and heir of Maximilian) should marry Juana, second daughter of Isabella and Ferdinand. A few months later another marriage was arranged; this was for the Infanta Catalina (known in English history as Catherine of Aragon) with Arthur, Prince of Wales, son of Henry VII of England.

Isabella's and Ferdinand's was indeed a tragic family.

Juan, the sovereigns' heir, during the celebrations of his marriage in Salamanca fell into a fever; Ferdinand hastened to his bedside to find his son – who was not quite twenty years of age – resigned to death.

Deeply concerned as to the effect this would have on Isabella who had always been a particularly fond parent, Ferdinand dared not break the news immediately, so caused several despatches to be sent to her, each preparing her for worse news to come.

There was general mourning throughout Spain at the death of the Prince of the Asturias; and hopes were centred on Juan's young wife, Margaret, who was pregnant.

But ill-fortune had already set in for the family. Margaret gave birth to a still-born child; and the heir to the throne of Spain was now Isabella (the sovereigns' eldest daughter) who had, much against her will, taken for her second husband Emanuel, King of Portugal. One of the conditions she had made before agreeing to the match was that Emanuel should expel all Jews from his dominion where many had taken refuge after the great exodus from Spain. Was this inspired by her parents, who in their turn had been inspired by Torquemada?

Emanuel, however, who was noted for his enlightened views, was very reluctant to bring in this measure which his intelligence told him was both harsh and foolish; but so eager was he for the match that he eventually consented.

The second daughter of Isabella and Ferdinand, Juana, who had married the ambitious Archduke Philip, was already noted for her eccentric manners; and it was a great grief to Isabella and Ferdinand when, inspired by her husband, she took the title of Princess of Castile thus implying that she considered herself heiress to the crown of Spain.

Isabella and Ferdinand then decided that their eldest daughter, Isabella of Portugal, should with her husband come at once to Castile that she might be publicly acclaimed as the heiress to her parents' crowns. They came in the spring of the year 1498. Young Isabella was pregnant, but her condition gave little cause for rejoicing for it seemed scarcely possible that she could have a satisfactory confinement.

The death of Juan hung over the family, and Isabella told her parents that she felt certain she could not survive the birth of her child.

She died in her mother's arms an hour after her son Miguel was born. Miguel himself died before he was two years old.

Now the next in succession to the throne was the eccentric Juana, much, there can be no doubt, to the satisfaction of her ambitious husband Archduke Philip.

Juana was to become insane, and the tragic history of Catalina, who was brought to England to marry Prince Arthur, and on his death married Prince Henry (who became Henry VIII) and was superseded in his affections by Anne Boleyn, is well known.

But in the year 1498 the sovereigns were mourning the deaths of Juan and Isabella; and it is a sign of the affection and respect they felt for Torquemada that they requested that the body of the Infante should be taken to Avila and buried there.

Perhaps an even greater sign of the favour in which the sovereigns held Torquemada was illustrated by the fact that, when it was necessary to send an embassy to England to negotiate for the marriage of Prince Arthur and Catalina, the arrangements for this embassy were put into the hands of the Inquisitor-General.

Torquemada, ever mindful of his beloved child, the Inquisition, sought to turn the occasion to advantage; he chose his embassy with care and sent with it a personal message to the King of England.

England was one of those countries into which the Inquisition had not entered, except on one isolated occasion (the persecution of the Templars by Edward II); that strip of Channel had been a barrier between the self-contained island and the rest of Europe, but now that a match was proposed between England and Spain, Torquemada was determined to take advantage of the situation, as he had (presumably) through the marriage of Isabella and Emanuel in Portugal by insisting on the exile of the Jews.

Henry VII was quite ready to make promises to further the match which he greatly desired. His shrewd mind would have been fully aware of the rising power of Spain; he was notorious for his miserly nature and naturally eager for the rich dowry which Catalina would bring to England.

The request, which reached him through Torquemada, was

that none who sought refuge from the Holy Office should be given it in England.

Torquemada's ambassador reported that Henry put both hands on his breast and swore an oath that he would persecute any heretic or Jew in his dominions to whom the Spanish authorities called his attention.

This compliance of the English sovereign must have brought a certain consolation to Torquemada, who would at this time have been feeling bitterly resentful towards Rome. Alexander had shown (as clearly as the suave Pontiff could) his lack of friendliness towards the Inquisitor-General; in addition he had shown a lack of respect for the methods of Torquemada in the *auto de fé* which was held in July 1498, in St Peter's Square, when a leniency had been shown towards heretics in direct contrast to the severe measures imposed by Torquemada's instructions. Torquemada had urged his sovereigns to protest to the Pontiff on account of the leniency displayed; to which Alexander blithely responded that he had forbidden the penitents to return to Spain without the permission of the sovereigns – implying thereby (still preserving that delightfully suave and most diplomatic manner) that what happened to them was no concern of Spain's. With such a man reigning in Rome, it was small wonder that Torquemada wished to make other allies, even as far afield as the island off the coast of Europe where the unpredictable Tudor dynasty had come into being.

So racked with pain was Torquemada during the last few years of his life that it might seem that a malicious fate was forcing him to suffer a little of the torment he had caused to be inflicted on so many. But if his body was reduced to inactivity, this was not the case with his mind.

Five months before his death he summoned the chief Inquisitors to Avila, and there he made known to them a further set of instructions which he had prepared for the procedure of the Inquisition.

This was the fourth set of instructions which Torquemada had produced, the others having been issued in 1484, 1485 and 1488. This last set, issued in May 1498, consisted of sixteen articles, the gist of which was:

1. Two Inquisitors were to be appointed to each court, and one of these must be a jurist, the other a theologian. They must not proceed separately to sentence a person to prison or to the torture; nor must they, except jointly, publish names of witnesses.

2. Officers of the Inquisition were not to be allowed to carry weapons in those places where the carrying of weapons was forbidden.

3. No person must be arrested unless there was good proof of guilt, and trials should be conducted with all possible speed, not (as had been the case in the affair of La Guardia) delayed in order to acquire damning evidence.

4. Actions against the dead should be conducted with promptitude, for delay caused great suffering to the children of such people, who were not allowed to marry while their parents' cases were *sub judice*.

5. Penances should not depend on the state of the Inquisition's exchequer, as had happened in the past. (When the Inquisition's funds were falling low, penances were increased.)

6. Corporal penance and imprisonment could not be excused on payment of fines; and only Inquisitors-General could give permission to discard the *sanbenito* and relieve children of the burden of their parents' sins.

7. Inquisitors must take great care in allowing reconciliation to those who confessed their sins *after* arrest, for when it was considered how long the Inquisition had been in operation, it would be seen that their sins had been committed out of sheer disobedience to the law, of which they must have been fully aware.

8. The Inquisition must severely and publicly prosecute all false witnesses.

9. In no tribunal should there be people who were related to each other, not only by blood but by course of business, such as masters or servants.

The remaining seven articles are concerned with matters of procedure and administration, such as the need for secrecy, the punishment of notaries who betray information, the setting up of courts of the Inquisition in territory as yet unexplored by them, and so on.

These were the last instructions of Torquemada, and on a casual examination it would appear that the spirit of the Grand Inquisitor had grown more kindly in his pain-racked body. But he was mainly concerned with the more efficient working of the Inquisition, and when the clauses are examined more closely they seem less kindly and certainly very revealing.

For instance when, as in Clause 3, Torquemada states that no person shall be arrested unless there is good proof of guilt, this means – as it always did – that people could be arrested providing the Inquisition consider there was sufficient proof. Their methods in the torture chambers with their *suspending* instead of *stopping* torture, and thus making it legal to pursue their hideous work, lay them open to suspicion in this respect. When names slipped from the mouths of men and women who were being submitted to the most acute agony in the torture chambers, it was considered sufficient proof and reason for arrest; so this clause, which sounds so kindly, is after all almost meaningless.

Clause 4 declares that actions against deceased persons should be conducted with great promptitude, that the children may not suffer. This again sounds as though a certain humanity was creeping into the mind of the Inquisitor-General. But at this time the corpse of almost every wealthy *converso* had been gruesomely exhumed and submitted to the faggots, and his wealth confiscated by the Inquisition.

The very fact that it should be necessary to warn against adjusting fines to the state of the exchequer gives a clear indication that nefarious practices had been pursued hitherto.

The article which states that false witnesses should be punished is also open to question. How could it be proved that a person had borne false witness when it was one of the laws of the Inquisition that the accused should not know who had accused them? The Inquisition had its own ideas of false witnesses, and these were not those who bore witness against the accused; they were those who denied knowledge of heresy in accused people whom the Inquisitors wished to condemn.

Yet it would seem at first glance that, in his last weeks on Earth, Torquemada had endeavoured to soften the harshness he had brought into being. He may have given the impression that he had done this, but his last Instructions smack of hypocrisy; one wonders whether he – who was so much the spirit of the Inquisition – was unconsciously deceiving himself. The Inquisition was his passion, his creation; he loved it tenderly; it was harsh, bitterly cruel, yet perhaps this man who saw himself as right, and all those who disagreed with him in the smallest detail wrong (not only wrong but wicked and undeserving of life) believed that the harshness was necessary. Yet how strange it is that, being on the point of death, he should have produced this set of Instructions which, on the surface (and the surface only) appear to show a glint of compassion – though perhaps that is too strong a word to use in connection with Torquemada. It is also characteristic. It remains in the tradition of that very spirit which created the Inquisition – arrogance, brutality, and an almost clinical cruelty, all carefully clothed in self-righteous anger and hypocrisy.

After completing the sixteen articles, Torquemada issued certain rules which the officers of the Inquisition were commanded to follow.

In these he laid down that no person was to visit prisoners of the Holy Office except those who brought them their food, and that such visitors must swear to preserve secrecy; examination of all the food which was taken to the prisoner must be made in order to search for any messages which some persons might have sought to convey to them. All officials must swear to remain silent concerning anything they had seen or heard within the prisons of the Inquisition. Should suspects be found guiltless and their goods restored, these goods must be restored in their full value at the time of confiscation; but any debts owed by the prisoners should be paid by the Inquisitors without consulting them.

If any property of condemned men had passed into other hands action should be taken to recover it.

Property confiscated from the condemned was to be sold after one month, but the receivers were not allowed to buy it; if they did so, and their fault was discovered, they would be fined as much as 100 ducats and, worse still, threatened with excommunication.

Inquisitors were bound to serve the Inquisition faithfully and were bound on oath to preserve secrecy; no gifts were to be accepted from prisoners, and if any were discovered breaking this law they would be subject to a heavy fine of as much as 100,000 maravidis and discharged from their Inquisitorial duties; and any who were aware that such a gift had been received by another and did not betray him would suffer a similar punishment.

It was further stressed that Inquisitors should never in any circumstances be alone with prisoners. They must never accept hospitality from New Christians but must pay for all they had; and all officers must hold only one post in the Inquisition and consequently receive only one salary.

There can be no doubt, when considering these new rules of Torquemada's, that he was aware of certain evil practices which were being carried on among the officers of the Inquisition, and these would naturally be deplored by a man such as Torquemada. Yet, because he was eager to prevent his servants from taking bribes, because he wished to institute in the Inquisition a mode of conduct which he could persuade himself was justice, this does not excuse him. Torquemada in those last weeks of his life, while suffering great bodily pain, was as eager as he had ever been to drive those who disagreed with him, through torture and fire, to salvation – according to the laws of the Church as laid down by himself.

These last instructions of Torquemada were a gesture to show the world that he and he alone remained supreme head of the Inquisition in Spain. Indomitable, he was in fiery action to the last. In May 1498 he issued his instructions; in July 1498 he, through the sovereigns, protested to Alexander VI concerning the famous *auto de fé* held in the square before St Peter's; and when the Pope's reply, which was a direct snub to the *Spanish* Inquisition, was received, Torquemada was dying.

On the 16th September, 1498, he died; he was buried in the chapel of the monastery which he himself had built. A simple stone above his tomb bore the inscription:

HIC JACET REVERENDUS P. F. THOMAS DE TURRE-CREMATA

PRIOR SANCTAE CRUCIS, INQUISITOR GENERALIS
HUJUS DOMUS FUNDATOR. OBIT ANNO DOMINI
MCDLXLVIII, DIE XVI SEPTEMBRIS.

It is impossible to stress too much the great effect this man
had on Spanish history. He had succeeded in releasing Spain
from Papal influence; he had played the biggest part in form-
ing this great and independent nation. He has been called the
Saviour of Spain; it is interesting to contemplate that his greatest effort, which was the setting up of the Inquisition, was to
contribute so largely to the downfall of that country.

His life presents – more than most others – the most striking
contrasts, so that while to many he is the Light of Spain and the
saviour of his country, to many more he is one of the cruellest
bigots who ever lived. Strangely enough both these assessments
have some truth in them. The unification of Spain and its rise
to temporal power were in a large measure due to him; and the
Spanish Inquisition, founded on his instructions, played a
significant part in bringing about the destruction of Spain's
greatness.

Those Catholic writers who seek to excuse his cruelty insist
that there have been gross exaggerations as to the number of
people who were burned at the stake during his rule. There may
have been exaggerations by Protestant writers, but one cannot
help feeling that the Catholics have been overwhelmingly
modest with their figures. Llorente states that between 1483
and 1498, while Torquemada was in command, 8,800 were
burned at the stake and 96,504 suffered less severe penalties.
Some historians put the figures at 10,000 burned by fire. Mich-
ael Ott, writing in the *Catholic Encyclopedia*, tells us that 'the
purity of the Christian Faith was in danger' and that the action
of Torquemada was necessary to preserve Spain. He also states
that only 2,000 were burned between the years 1481 and 1504,
when Isabella died.

23

Perhaps the figures of Llorente can be treated with greater respect than those which appear excessively high or low. Many *autos* took place between 1483 and 1498, and many people suffered the supreme penalty; moreover Llorente was working from the records of the Inquisition itself and it appears that he writes with calm integrity, allowing for occasional lapses into righteous anger, which any normal person would feel against great cruelty.

Philip II, whose admiration for Torquemada can be well understood – for there is much which is similar in their natures – had the remains of the Inquisitor-General removed from their humble grave and re-interred in a place of honour in the Cathedral.

They were taken from this resting-place in 1836, when the tomb was rifled, and were then scattered.

Thus Torquemada, who had caused suffering to so many, died in bodily misery; and he, who had caused many to be taken from their graves that their remains might be humiliated, had the same treatment accorded to his bones.

CHAPTER TWO

THE RISE OF XIMENES

If there was another person during the reign of Isabella and Ferdinand who had as great an effect on Spain's history as Torquemada that person was surely Cardinal Ximenes; and it is an interesting fact that these two men – the former a Dominican, the latter a Franciscan and both Inquisitors-General – should be of such similar characters. Though perhaps this is to be expected, for Ferdinand, Isabella and the newly-born Spain could make use of such men; and it was doubtless for this reason that Torquemada and Ximenes did more than any others to set the new course and carry Spain along the journey she was to take.

Ximenes (Gonzalo Ximenes de Cisneros) was born in Torrelaguna, a small village close to Madrid, in the year 1436, and as in the case of Torquemada it was during his later life that he did the work which was to give him a place in history.

He was thirty-seven when he came into such conflict with the Primate of Spain, Carillo, Archbishop of Toledo, that he leaped into prominence.

Carillo, who was an uncle of the Marquis of Villena, a favourite of John II, had in his turn played a certain part in the politics of Castile, for he was a prelate who was more suited to the battlefield than to the Church. A strong man, he was excessively proud; his friendship was important to the peace of the monarch, and his enmity was to be feared. Poor weak Henry IV was to discover this to his cost when Carillo, with the help of the disgruntled Villena, sought to depose him and set up his young half-brother Alfonso in his place. Later, on the death of Alfonso, he had given his support to Isabella, but since he was a man ever on the look-out for slights which would impair his dignity, he eventually began to plot against Isabella; and he rode into battle side by side with Alfonso of Portugal who had come to fight for the crown of Castile on behalf of Henry's illegitimate daughter, La Beltraneja, whom he (Alfonso) planned to marry and with whom he hoped to share the throne.

When the Portuguese armies were beaten Carillo was forced to sue for pardon, which was granted by the victorious Isabella in exchange for a large portion of his estates.

After such disasters Carillo was forced to retire to Alcalá de Henares, where he spent his remaining years in the study of alchemy, which he pursued so earnestly that he dissipated a large part of his fortunes. There he died and was succeeded as Primate of Spain by Pedro Gonzalez de Mendoza, who had long been a rival.

Mendoza was the fourth son of the Marquis de Santillana; he was extremely talented and not content to work only within the limits of the Church. Like Carillo, he wished to take a place in politics; and even during the reign of Henry IV he sought to ingratiate himself with Isabella. It may have been that his foresight assured him that Isabella would one day be the Queen of Castile and that it would be wise to throw in his lot with her. If this were so he was certainly proved to be right.

The character of Mendoza was in striking contrast to that of Ximenes and Torquemada; he was a lover of luxury, and the pomp and magnificence of high office appealed greatly to him. He had not allowed his position in the Church to interfere with those carnal pleasures in which he indulged so freely, and he was the father of several illegitimate children.

The Cardinal's nature was tolerant. This is shown by an occasion when a priest, in his presence, was bold enough to deliver a sermon on the morals of high churchmen, which was clearly aimed at Mendoza. The Cardinal's followers wished to punish the preacher for his insolence, but Mendoza declared that all preachers had a right to state their views, and would not allow the priest to be touched. He himself sent him a gift of game, accompanied by a large sum of money, as reward for his boldness. But although Mendoza recognized the preacher's right to state his opinions, he claimed the right to live according to his own desires; and the words of warning delivered from the pulpit had no effect on his way of living.

When Carillo died and Mendoza succeeded him as Arch-bishop of Toledo he found greater scope for action in that field which had always attracted him: politics.

His pleasure-loving easy-going nature made him oppose the new laws which Torquemada wished to introduce into the In-quisition, and it was due in some measure to him that the delay occurred between the sanction of Sixtus IV and the setting up of the Inquisition in Spain, much to the irritation of Ojeda and Torquemada. It was Mendoza who prepared the Catechism (*Catecismo de la Doctrina Cristiana*) in an attempt to stave off the introduction of the new Inquisition.

Events moved in favour of Torquemada and Ojeda, and Mendoza could do nothing but join with Torquemada and ap-point Juan de San Martin and Miguel Morillo as the In-quisitors of Seville.

Mendoza – more interested in matters of state than of the Church – played such a big part in politics that he became known at Court as The Third King of Spain; and when the armies were before Granada, Mendoza was there at the head of a detachment of troops; and he was with the sovereigns when they entered the fallen city.

It was Mendoza who supported Christopher Columbus when he was seeking Isabella's help in fitting him out for his voyage of discovery, and who was largely responsible for turning the Queen's opinion in the explorer's favour.

Cultured, aristocratic and greatly talented, the Cardinal con-tinued to hold favour until his death; and when he was dying Isabella ordered that the Court move near to Guadalaxara, where he lay, that she might visit him frequently and in person.

As Mendoza lay on his death-bed Isabella discussed with him the difficult task of appointing his successor; and Mendoza warned her emphatically against selecting him from the nobil-ity. Archbishops of Toledo were the Primates of Spain and, calling attention to the arrogance of his predecessor, Carillo, Mendoza pointed out the danger of appointing a member of the nobility who had a powerful family and riches behind him.

It was at this time that Mendoza suggested that the man best suited to the post was the Queen's confessor, Fray Gonzalo Ximenes de Cisneros.

Ximenes came from a family which, although in the past it may have been affluent, was, at the time of his birth, in humble circumstances. When he came to fame an illustrious ancestry was provided for him by those who thought it was necessary that he should have it, but it is not possible to say how much truth there is in legends such as that of a maternal ancestor, de la Torre, who was a famous duellist of the tenth century and who eventually restored Madrid to the Castilians.

He was destined for the priesthood at a very early age and accordingly was sent first to Salamanca and then to Alcalá de Henares where he studied canon and civil law.

The family was poor and he had two brothers, John and Bernardín, whose future must be thought of; therefore it was decided that Gonzalo would have a better chance of advancement in Rome; and he accordingly set out for that city.

He stayed there for five years, and nothing is known of his progress there except that he practised as an advocate; and when his father died he decided he should return to his home, but he must have distinguished himself by his service in Rome because, when he left, he was given a Papal Bull (*expectative*) which offered him the first benefice of value to fall vacant; and as his native village of Torrelaguna was in Toledo, he chose Toledo; and it was his choice of Toledo which was to bring him into conflict with Carillo.

It was some years after his return when the Archpriest of Uzeda died and the vacancy occurred; Ximenes immediately took possession of it. Not that it was an important benefice; it was, however situated in that spot where Ximenes had chosen to live, and with the Papal permission in his pocket he felt himself justified in taking it.

The Sovereigns had always resented Papal interference in their country, and the arrogant Carillo, Archbishop of Toledo, was furious not only on account of the Pope's high-handed behaviour but because he, Carillo, had promised the benefice to a friend. He therefore demanded that Ximenes abandon the benefice without delay. This Ximenes refused to do, and as a result Carillo descended on him in fury; and since he refused to leave his post he was removed by force and imprisoned in the fortress of Uzeda. There, Carillo believed he would realize the folly of setting himself against the high officials of the Church in Spain and learn to understand that Papal influence could do little to extricate him from the predicament in which he found himself.

Ximenes however remained obstinate and continued to assert that the benefice was his, since it had been granted by Pope Paul II.

The furious Carillo then removed him from Uzeda to Santorcaz, which was a fortress used to imprison recalcitrant members of the Church. Carillo kept him in this prison for six years and then suddenly released him. Ximenes' release is said to have been brought about by the intervention of Carillo's niece, the Countess of Buendia, although why this lady should have interested herself in the priest is not known. However, released he was, and realizing that he could hope for little in Toledo where Carillo held sway he found a vacancy in Sigüenza and became a chaplain there. In this post he had his first stroke of good fortune, for Mendoza was then Bishop of Sigüenza.

Mendoza recognized the unusual intellectual powers of the chaplain immediately – and it was possible that he was interested in a man who had stood up so valiantly to his, Mendoza's, great rival, Carillo; however Mendoza selected Ximenes for special favours and very quickly made him Vicar General of the diocese.

Mendoza shortly afterwards became Archbishop of Seville, and Ximenes carried on in Sigüenza; he became noted not only for his ecclesiastical learning and skill but for his business ability, and when the Count of Cifuentes was taken prisoner by the Moors he asked that Ximenes might be allowed to look after his estates, which were in the diocese.

Ximenes was now on the road to fortune, but stern priest that he was, following devotedly in the footsteps of Torquemada, he had no wish for secular triumphs, and he decided to enter the most austere of all monastic orders, the Observatine Franciscans.

When St Francis died there had been a division of opinion in the order he had founded. Many of his followers believed that they should adhere strictly to the rules laid down by St Francis; but many others, finding these too rigorous and seeing little virtue in torturing their bodies and suffering hardship and discomfort, insisted that it was enough to live in their monastery and pray at certain times. Therefore there was a split and the two sects decided to go their own ways. It was with the Observatines, who lived the rigorous life, that Ximenes chose to live.

So he entered the Convent of San Juan de los Reyes at Toledo. This had been newly erected as a result of a vow which Ferdinand and Isabella had made during the siege of Granada; and here Ximenes gave himself fervently to the life of austerity. He abandoned the name he had been given at his birth – Gonzalo – and took that of the founder of the Order, Francisco. He refused to sleep in a bed and chose the floor with a plank for his pillow. He constantly suffered the discomfort of the hair-shirt, and vied with St Francis himself in the privations to which he subjected his body.

His fame began to spread, and many rich and powerful people invited him to become their confessor or to advise them on their spiritual problems; so finding himself beset on all sides by worldly matters he begged his superiors for permission to go into retreat.

As a result he set out for Our Lady of Casañar, a convent which was so called because of the forest of chestnut trees in the midst of which it was situated. Within the convent there was great privacy; but Ximenes yearned for the life of a hermit and, again with the permission of his superiors, he went out into the forest to live in complete solitude. He built himself a hut – rough and so small that it was only big enough to contain his person, and here he lived on bread and water for days at a time and in all weathers. He spent hours on his knees in the forest; and it is said that his fellow Franciscans sometimes came upon him in a trance lying on the ground or in a kneeling posture.

It seems that during the years Ximenes spent in the solitude

30

of the forest he was seeking self-knowledge. He would appear to have been a man of deeper spiritual conscience than Torquemada. Ximenes was aware of the ambition which was strong within him. A man of the Church he wished to be, but he also possessed a great desire for power. It may have been that he found it more difficult to deceive himself that Torquemada had. He had been given the Papal Bull almost certainly at his own request. Why should he have asked for it if he had not hopes of rising in his profession; and why should he have insisted on taking it when Carillo had sought to withhold it? Why had he in the first place gone to Rome? Because there was more chance of advancement there. This all points to ambition. And the reason Ximenes fled from his growing power in Sigüenza could have been because he was discovering within himself an overwhelming love of that power.

He was clearly being pulled in two directions – towards obscurity and sanctity such as he felt he could achieve in the convent of Our Lady of Castañar and towards ambition which he knew could be satisfied because of his undoubted talents. He had come to know Mendoza, Bishop of Sigüenza, soon to be Archbishop of Seville and shortly after that to aspire to the highest place of all, the Archbishopric of Toledo, and he would have seen in his benefactor a man such as he himself might easily become. Might it not have been because of this that he shut himself away in the convent and the lonely hut in the forest so that he might purge himself of all wordly desires and increase that spirituality after which he was straining?

He spent three years of acute austerity and meditation at Our Lady of Castañar, and at the end of that time his superiors decided that there was work he could do for the Order in the Convent of Salzeda, where he was made Superior. In his new role he insisted on continuing in his humility and himself undertook menial tasks such as sweeping the floors. Like Torquemada he was by nature arrogant and possessed of great pride. Unlike Torquemada he was aware of these characteristics and continually sought to repress them.

He was at Salzeda in that fateful year 1492; and with the conquest of Granada Isabella bestowed the title Archbishop of

Granada on her confessor, Fray Fernando de Talavera; thus Isabella found herself in need of a confessor, and asked the advice of Mendoza as to whom she should appoint. Mendoza, at that time Archbishop of Toledo, and Primate of Spain – a post which he had held since the death of Carillo ten years before – immediately thought of Ximenes.

Mendoza believed that Ximenes was too brilliant to spend his life in a convent; there was no need, because he was a Franciscan, to cut himself off from affairs of state. Mendoza had never allowed his connection with the Church to shut him off from politics. He was fully aware that the Queen's confessor had a double part to play. It had been thus with Talavera and Torquemada before him. Ximenes was a man who could be trusted to look after Isabella's secular problems as well as her soul.

As a result of Mendoza's recommendation Isabella sent for Ximenes and, knowing a great deal about the man through what she had heard from Mendoza, she did not at first tell him why she had sent for him. She was impressed by his calm manners; and his wasted body and pallid looks bore witness to his saintly habits.

She thereupon decided that he should take Talavera's place, and must have been astonished when Ximenes received the news with dismay.

His new post meant that his prospects were excellent; as Queen's confessor he would have every opportunity of gaining influence over her, but Ximenes had no wish to rise in the world outside his convent and he made it a condition of accepting the Queen's offer that he should be able to retire there when his presence was not required at Court.

It was not long before Isabella was putting the utmost trust in her confessor.

Two years later Ximenes was made Provincial of the Franciscan Order in Castile, and this gave him the opportunity he needed to act against the Conventuals, that branch of the Franciscans whose members had not followed in the footsteps of their founder but had sought the less rigorous life.

He continued to live in the utmost austerity and, when he went about the country visiting the various Franciscan monasteries in accordance with his new role, he always travelled on foot in abject humility, begging his way as he went. Often he would be accompanied by Fray Francisco Ruiz who was his faithful friend (according to some records, his nephew) and whom he subsequently made Bishop of Avila.

Ximenes made complaints to the Queen about the manner in which the Conventuals lived. Many of them had large estates where they enjoyed great splendour and indulged in amorous adventure.

Isabella was sympathetic, and prevailed upon the Pope (Alexander VI) to issue a Bull which would give Ximenes permission to introduce the reforms he sought. Ximenes got to work with that zeal which he was later to use in the service of the Inquisition, and those monks who would not fall into line were expelled from their monasteries.

Shortly after this work was begun Mendoza became very ill and it appeared that the highest post in Spain under the King and Queen was about to fall vacant; for not only did the Archbishopric of Toledo carry with it the post of Primate but also that of the Grand Chancellorship of Castile (thus providing temporal as well as spiritual power).

Greatly impressed by the high moral character of her confessor and having heard him recommended from the dying lips of a man whose judgment she had always trusted, Isabella was inclined to nominate Ximenes for the post.

Ferdinand however had a candidate. This was his illegitimate son Alfonso, whom he had made Archbishop of Saragossa when the boy was six years old.

Isabella was a woman who believed firmly in the sanctity of the family; she was exceedingly jealous where her husband was concerned, and the lusty Ferdinand had given her cause enough for such jealousy. Yet, had she believed the choice of young Alfonso to have been a wise one, she might have granted her husband's request. Mendoza had recommended Ximenes and he had also warned her against choosing one who had powerful family connections.

Isabella could be very firm; and one imagines her conveying to her wayward husband, who not only was unfaithful enough to have a son by another woman two years after his marriage to Isabella, but bold enough to ask his wife for favours for that son, that she and she alone was mistress of Castile and would herself decide all important matters such as this one.

She therefore sent to Alexander VI asking him to confirm her nomination of Ximenes as Archbishop of Toledo, and when the Papal Bull arrived she summoned Ximenes to her presence.

It was Good Friday of the year 1495, and she allowed Ximenes to hear her confession before she handed him the Bull which had arrived from the Vatican.

It was addressed: 'To our venerable son, Francisco Ximenes de Cisneros, Archbishop-elect of Toledo.'

When Ximenes read those words he was astounded, for it was the first intimation he had had that he was being considered for the honour. One wonders what his true feelings were when he realized what was being offered to him. He must have felt that the devil was showing him the kingdoms of the world. His first reaction was the need to escape – which might be an indication of the greatness of the temptation. He dropped the letter, murmured that there had been a mistake and, before the Queen could speak, rushed out of her presence in a manner which must have bordered on *lèse-majesté*.

Isabella was not displeased. She could assess the worth of this man and she had learned to trust him. As he did not return she sent servants after him to command him to come to her presence.

When Ximenes came back Isabella argued with him, but again and again he refused the honour, declaring himself to be unfit for and unworthy of it.

For six months he held out against his advisers and the Queen's desire, but when another Bull arrived from the Vatican, commanding him to take the appointment which the Church had sanctioned, he gave in.

He was then sixty years old.

On October 11th of that year, 1495, he was consecrated at Tarazona, became Archbishop of Toledo, Chancellor of Castile

34

and Primate of Spain; and from that day for the next twenty-two years he retained his high office and was thus able to escape but rarely from the world of affairs into the seclusion of his hermit's hut.

CHAPTER THREE

THE POWER OF XIMENES

The ardour with which Ximenes pursued those defaulters among the Franciscans gave a clue to how much more zealous he would be in the extirpation of heretics.

He had subdued his own flesh to such an extent that he could have little sympathy for the suffering of others. Pain and even life on Earth would seem to him of little account; the sole purpose in being on Earth, in the estimation of such men as he, was to prepare for the life hereafter. Happiness to these men was in itself a sin – laughter, gaiety, pleasure were the hand-maidens of the devil, and to enjoy them oneself or to allow them to others savoured of mortal sin. In place of happiness they put self-righteousness, contentment with their own state, their certainty of a place in heaven. Arrogance was the key to their character, and men such as Torquemada and Ximenes contained more of this characteristic than those such as the Borgia Pope himself, who made no secret of their love of worldly pomp and pleasure.

Following the tolerant Mendoza it was natural that Ximenes should quickly become unpopular. The nobles were disconcerted that a man of humble origin should have been chosen to fill the highest position under the Sovereigns; the Conventuals already had their grudge against him; and there must surely have been that suspicion of him amongst countless others which is certain to rest upon one who, by his austere conduct and ultra-pious habits, sets himself apart from his fellow men.

The facts that Ximenes could not be reached through bribes, and did not care whom he offended, did not endear him to the Court. His wasted frame and gaunt figure would have been a continual reminder to others of their own self-indulgence. Saints cannot expect to be popular amongst sinners. And although some of us today, looking back on the picture over almost five hundred years, see quite clearly that Ximenes was no saint, he might have appeared so to those who could not look as we can – beyond the outward performance. Today many people would define a saint as one who had acquired the gift of self-effacement and self-sacrifice; we are not inclined to attach the label to those who, by submitting their bodies to privation here on Earth, imagine they are preparing it for a state of glorification in a life to come. Their motive is entirely selfish, and selfishness and saintliness cannot go hand in hand. And as to some of us it appears that these medieval saints never seemed to be content with harming their own bodies but continually sought to lead others to their own brand of salvation by torturing them, we question their claim to sainthood.

In addition to the rancour, irritation and envy which Ximenes aroused in so many about him, there was also the resentment of Ferdinand himself who, naturally enough, could not forget that this man had been preferred to his own son; it would have been asking too much of a man like Ferdinand to give wholehearted support to the new Primate. Ximenes may not have helped their relationship by never swerving from his loyalty to the King, for there must have been times when the more human Ferdinand would have welcomed a little resentment of certain slights he himself could not resist offering the new Archbishop of Toledo.

Ximenes was determined to pursue what he believed to be the righteous path, and he made this very clear from the beginning. Mendoza had appointed his brother, Pedro Hurtado de Mendoza, to be Governor of Cazorla. This governorship was one of great prestige and with it went a considerable fortune. As the Cardinal had been responsible for the rise to power of Ximenes it seemed natural that Ximenes should show his gratitude in his behaviour towards the Mendoza family, and naturally enough all expected the new Archbishop to confirm the young Mendoza's appointment.

The Mendoza family and their friends did not hesitate, when Ximenes seemed in no hurry to assure the young Mendoza that his appointment was secure, to remind the Archbishop of all the great Cardinal had done for him. Ximenes was on his mettle, declaring that he neither sought favours nor gave them. As Archbishop of Toledo he considered himself free to act in accordance with his own conscience, and if he were not so, he would have no hesitation in resigning immediately.

There was consternation throughout the Mendoza family. As for Isabella, she looked on with approval at the conduct of her new Archbishop.

However, Ximenes did not mean to withhold the rich post from the brother of his friend, but merely to show that he gave no favours. Shortly afterwards, he took an opportunity of meeting the young Mendoza at a public function, where he greeted him as Governor of Cazorla. Thus he proclaimed that he had selected the man whom he believed most suited to the post, and that the appointment had nothing to do with friendship.

In a world where nepotism was so flagrantly practised by the heads of the Church, this new attitude was particularly astonishing. It brought consternation to many, but those who profited by it or in spite of it (such as Pedro Hurtado de Mendoza) applauded it, and the young Mendoza became as ardent a supporter of Ximenes as his brother had been.

It is interesting to look at Ximenes' relationship with his own brother. Bernardín had joined the Franciscan Order and Ximenes had made him a steward in his own household. One wonders how the appointment fitted in with Ximenes' rigorous determination to eschew nepotism, for Bernardín, judging from his conduct, was certainly not worthy of the honour bestowed on him.

Ximenes probably felt that he had a duty to this young brother and gave him the post that he might keep his eye on him. Often he lectured the younger man on his lack of virtue, and again and again Bernardín left his brother's household for his monastery, preferring the life there to living perpetually under the eye of austerity. Bernardín's conduct became so tiresome that he imprisoned him for a few months; afterwards however, he took him back to his role of steward.

Bernardín, feigning repentance, felt none and, when

Ximenes was ill, he, professing to speak on behalf of his brother, prevailed upon an ecclesiastical court to give a judgment which was unjust. Ximenes, who was very angry, sent for his brother in order to rebuke him; but looking at that wraith of a man lying feebly on his pillows Bernardín lost his head; he might be morally weak, but he was physically strong. He pushed his brother back onto his pillows and, taking one from under him, pressed it down over Ximenes' face. Had not the attention of one of the servants been attracted by the scuffle, Ximenes might have been murdered by his brother.

Ximenes sent Bernardín back to his monastery, gave him a small pension, and never saw him again. His conduct towards his own brother was certainly more lenient than it was towards others.

His unpopularity persisted and it was stronger than ever amongst the Franciscans, who had expected favours to fall into their laps when one of their number was elevated to such high office. Those whom he took into his household found that they were no better off than they had been in their monasteries, for as Ximenes himself accepted no bribes, he certainly would not allow those who served him to do so.

Several of them sent a deputation to the General of their Order in Rome, and as a result the General came to Isabella with a complaint against the new Archbishop. He happened to belong to the Conventuals and was angered by the monastic reforms which Ximenes was trying to bring about.

In Isabella's presence this man ranted against Ximenes to whom he referred as an upstart without noble blood in his veins, a hypocrite whose assumed piety cloaked his ambition. He demanded that the Queen remove him at once from his high office.

Was he mad, demanded Isabella, or did he not realize to whom he was speaking?

The General, furious beyond discretion, cried out that he was fully aware whom he addressed. She was Isabella, Queen of Castile – a mere handful of dust, as he himself was. With that he hurried from the Queen's presence.

The visit of the General did nothing whatever to turn Isabella's loyalty from her new Archbishop. She was determined to support him whenever possible and to protect him from his enemies – even from such a powerful one as her own husband, Ferdinand – for she felt she understood what underlay their enmity towards him.

Now Ximenes had become so powerful it would seem that his attitude had undergone a change. He had been reluctant to assume that power; now it was his, he was even more reluctant to relinquish any part of it.

When those who were alarmed at his increasing reforms decided to send an emissary to the Pope to complain about him, Ximenes was determined to intercept the messenger. The man chosen for this delicate task was a certain Albornoz, and as soon as Ximenes heard he had set out, the Archbishop sent one of his men to the coast to arrest him. Ximenes' man arrived too late, for Albornoz had already set sail for Italy; however the official also took ship and arrived on the coast of Italy before Albornoz who, on touching Italian soil, was arrested and brought back as a prisoner of state. He was put in prison where he remained for nearly two years – time enough to meditate on the folly of seeking to work against the powerful Archbishop of Toledo.

Ximenes' energetic conduct in the matter showed quite clearly how determined he was to keep his power. No doubt he believed, as Torquemada had believed, that he could use that power to the glory of God. It is impossible for us to decide – as indeed it may have been for Ximenes himself – how much this power was desired for the glorification of the man himself.

Complaints however did reach Alexander in Rome. The new Archbishop brought no dignity to his office, it was said. He walked about in garments patched by himself. The high office had lost prestige since those days when it had been held by that aristocrat the Cardinal Mendoza.

Alexander, that lover of gaiety and pomp, magnificence and splendour, could well understand the irritation Ximenes must be causing.

According to Alvaro Gomez de Castro, who was born in 1515, (2 years before the death of Ximenes) and who provides the main source of information concerning him, Alexander wrote in the following strain to the Archbishop: 'Dear Brother, the Holy and Universal Church, as you are aware, like heavenly Jerusalem, has many and diverse adornments. It is wrong to seek them too vehemently, and it is also wrong to reject them with contempt. Each state has certain conditions which are suited to it, and which please God and are therefore to be praised. All – and especially prelates – should eschew arrogance by too much display, and superstition by too much humility. In both cases the Church may be weakened. We advise and urge you to live according to the rank which you hold; the Holy Father has raised you from humble state to that of Archbishop, and although you should live in your conscience according to the rules of God (and this we applaud) in your external life you should maintain the dignity of your rank.'

Such admonition, diplomatically couched as it was, was a command; and, coming from such a quarter, one which Ximenes could not ignore. Thereafter he wore the brilliant garments of his rank, but always under them was the rough vest of the Franciscan, and beneath that the hair shirt. These he mended with his own hands. He set up an elaborate bed in his chamber, but beneath this was the pallet on which he lay each night.

He was determined to live as the hermit had lived in the forest about Our Lady of Castañar; but, in place of the hermit who sought solitude that he might meditate and come to greater spiritual understanding, there was growing the reformer.

When the town of Granada had surrendered to the Christian Armies which were laying siege to it, the last Moorish King, Boabdil (who has been often condemned for his weakness) secured very favourable terms for the Moors. These terms related mainly to religion, and in them it was set out that the people of Granada were to keep their mosques and be allowed to follow their own religion.

These terms had been strictly adhered to for the eight years which followed the surrender of the city, and as a result peace reigned in Granada.

Isabella had no wish to make trouble; Ferdinand was rarely

concerned with religion unless such concern could bring material benefits. He was in favour of the Inquisition mainly because it brought large revenues to the exchequer.

At the time of the fall of Granada Isabella had appointed two men to look after the affairs of the city. One of these was a member of the Mendoza family, the Count of Tendilla, and the other was Talavera, who was made Archbishop of Granada.

The Count of Tendilla had been made alcayde and captain-general of Granada on its fall and was in charge of the civil administration; Talavera, who had been Bishop of Avila, had been given the archiepiscopal See of Granada at the same time.

Tendilla, a wise man and one who was not intolerant for his time, was a good choice on the part of Isabella and Ferdinand. Talavera, who was of humble origin and had been a Hieronymite monk in the monastery of Santa Maria del Prado for twenty years before he became the Queen's confessor, was learned and modest, although something of a bigot. But both Tendilla and Talavera, being aware of the conditions made at the time of the surrender, were determined to carry them out for the honour of Spain; and thus during almost eight years since the Moorish capital had come under the domination of Ferdinand and Isabella, harmonious conditions had prevailed within the city.

Ximenes however could not tolerate the thought of the Infidels' following their own religion within the kingdom; and when the Court travelled to Granada, and Ximenes went with it, he determined to convert the Moors to Christianity. Thus a situation was arising very similar to that which had brought disaster to the Jews who had become New Christians. The place of the Jews in the tragedy about to be enacted was to be taken by the Moors.

Since the expulsion of the Jews in 1492, the Inquisition had been busy, and every Jew in Spain was suspect for, by the very nature of the exodus, he must be a *converso*. Torquemada's last instructions, issued in 1498 – only a year before the journey of Ximenes to Granada – showed clearly that the Inquisition was in need of reform. Mussulmans were outside its scope since they could not be persecuted for heresy; therefore if the In-

42

quisition needed more victims, here was an untapped source waiting for it. If the Mussulmans were forced to baptism they would be as vulnerable as the converted Jews; they could be smelt out for following old Moorish customs as the Jews had been for following theirs. Quite clearly there must have been many enthusiastic supporters of the Inquisition who were eager to force baptism on the Moors.

When Ximenes came into Granada he questioned Talavera on the state of affairs there and was eager that more should be done to bring about the conversion of the Moors. When the Court moved on to Seville he stayed behind. Isabella and Ferdinand however reminded him of the treaty which had been made before Granada and, knowing the zeal of their Primate, impressed on him the need to give no offence to the Moors.

Talavera had learnt Arabic and had had certain books translated into that language in the hope of bringing about greater understanding between Mussulmans and Christians. Both he and Mendoza had not spared themselves in trying to convert the Moors to Christianity. But their methods, Ximenes insisted, were not active enough. He himself would set about the reformation of the city.

He began by inviting many of the *alfaquis* to meet him; he presented them with gifts of rich silk and red hats, for the Moors delighted to adorn themselves with fine clothes; he then began to lecture them on the superiority of the Christian religion. The Moors, no doubt delighted with the red hats and bales of silk, wished to please the kind bringer of gifts, and many did as he asked and accepted baptism. Many more came to the meeting place, for they had heard of the rich presents which were being given away; and indeed Ximenes is said to have impoverished himself by the amount of gifts he was obliged to bestow.

There were however many wise men among the Moors who were growing uneasy. They did not forget the existence of the Inquisition. They had arranged that it should not enter Granada; nor could it if the Moors had remained Mussulmans and the Spanish Sovereigns had kept faith. They saw that this was the beginning of trouble. They were not, it was true, being

43

forced to accept baptism; but this fiery Archbishop of Toledo, with his eloquence and gifts, was perhaps not strictly carrying out the spirit of the contract. Day after day men and women were being coerced into accepting the Christian Faith; they did not seem to be aware of what could happen to those who were baptized and then, perhaps innocently, reverted in any way to their own faith.

The shadow of that grim monster, the Inquisition, had been kept so far from Granada, that these people did not realize, as they joyously set their new red hats on their heads, that they were opening the gates of the city to a force, the evil power of which they could not begin to understand until they had experienced it.

One of the Moors, a learned *alfaquis* named Zegri, who was regarded with great respect by his countrymen, came to see Ximenes and was unimpressed by all the gifts and eloquence. Losing patience with him and realizing that if he could convert him he would bring hundreds more to baptism (and if he did not the *alfaquis* might influence his flock against Christianity), Ximenes made him a prisoner and told the official who took him away to take such measures as would bring Zegri out of his ignorance.

Zegri was submitted to rigorous confinement, was made to fast and kept in fetters; and after a period of this treatment he declared that Allah had visited him in a vision and commanded him to become a Christian.

As Ximenes had expected, the example set by Zegri was followed by hundreds of the Moors of Granada, for tension, which had not been there before the coming of Ximenes, had crept into the city.

Ximenes was acting contrary to the Treaty of Granada for his bigotry had come between him and his sense of justice. He could see nothing wrong in breaking a treaty if as a result he could force the citizens of Granada into submission. He determined to destroy the Moslem Faith in Spain. At this time he was as fanatical as Torquemada had ever been concerning the Jews. He knew that the learned members of the Moorish population were deeply disturbed by what was going on; they had

44

built up during their years in Spain a great literature; and literature is naturally feared by all tyrants. Ximenes decided that no writings in Arabic should exist in the city of Granada, and he sent out an order that all books, manuscripts and any forms of Arabic writing were to be brought out and placed in piles in the great squares of the city.

The making of books had been perfected by the Spanish Arabs as by no other people in Europe; they could produce magnificent bindings, and illustrated beautifully. The books were of the greatest value, yet that did not save them.

Ximenes received the books and from them selected three hundred which dealt with medical science, in which the Moors excelled; these he preserved for the university of Acalá, which he was building, for since they did not deal with religion they were considered to be untainted.

The rest – thousands of them – he caused to be burned, irrespective of their value, and their religious significance to the Moors.

As the smoke rose upwards it would have seemed that here was a grim warning to the people of Granada. Their first *auto de fé*. On this occasion it was books which were burned. There would be other occasions when human flesh would take the place of books. And the man who had commanded the burning of books and was presiding over the melancholy scene, was the Inquisitor-General.

Fortunately many people had not given up their books, and some were smuggled out of the country; but the loss was felt in the centuries to come and, being deprived of their literature, the Arabs were robbed of their culture; and this became apparent in the years ahead.

It was not only Moors who looked on at this distressing scene with dismay and disgust; men such as Tendilla and Talavera warned Ximenes that he was going too far; they reminded him of the treaty, and that those who had been forced to receive baptism could not be true Christians. Ximenes had an answer to that. Temporal matters might be served by mildness, he retorted, not so the saving of souls. Unbelievers should be forced to accept salvation if they would not accept it willingly;

and at such a time when Mohammedanism was shaken to its roots, he should relentlessly pursue the course he had taken.

Perhaps he was also thinking of that organization which knew very well how to deal with those who became converted and relapsed into the old evil ways. Torquemada had shown the way with the Jews; Ximenes would show the way with the Moors.

It was not to be expected that the Moors could stand placidly by and watch with equanimity the destruction of their national culture; and when Ximenes sent three of his servants into the Albaycin (that section of the city which was inhabited solely by the Moorish population) they were received with a sullenness which was ominous. These men had been assiduous in the service of their master and had worked with him in his proselytizing. A quarrel was picked with them and, as a result, two of Ximenes' servants were assassinated; the other managed to escape.

Now the fury of the Moors was aroused and they were determined to drive from their city those who had interfered so disastrously with their peace. The leaders of the insurrection went through the streets calling all the servants of Allah to take arms. In a very short time the whole of the Albaycin was ready for action.

An avenging party made its way into the city to that palace where Ximenes was lodged. The servants of Ximenes were alarmed for his safety, for they knew how deeply he was abhorred for his actions, and begged him to escape at once to the Alhambra where the Count of Tendilla (whose liberal and tolerant rule had made the Arabs regard him as their friend) could, if any could, save him from the fury of the mob.

Ximenes however was no coward. His conduct had brought about this insurrection and he was ready to take the consequences. Perhaps the hermit of Our Lady of Castañar believed that the martyr's crown was about to descend upon his head, and welcomed it. He would see great virtue in his conduct, which had brought unhappiness to many Mussulmans, for he was undoubtedly possessed of that blind faith which made him see his own bigotry as virtue to be rewarded in heaven by his God who, made in his own image, would be as arrogant a bigot, as indifferent to the suffering of others, as he was himself.

He would not, he declared, think of his own safety, for so many of the true faith were putting theirs in danger.

His palace was a strong one, and his guards capable of its defence; moreover a message had been conveyed to the Count of Tendilla who made with all haste to succour Ximenes. The sight of the Count, who had won the trust of the Moors, at the head of a strong contingent, was enough to send the Moors back to the Albaycin.

However, the Moorish blood was up. They were not going to submit willingly to further persecution; and although they returned to their quarters in the city they were still in a mood of rebellion; their purpose was to drive Ximenes out of their city.

The situation was saved by those two who had the confidence of the anxious Mussulmans – Tendilla and Talavera – and they, with great bravery, went into the Albaycin, into the heart of the revolt, to attempt to make peace. First came Talavera with a few of his servants, all of them unarmed; his chaplain led the way, carrying the cross before him.

As the crowds saw these brave men coming among them, they ceased to shout for vengeance on the Christian meddlers. The Moors were great respecters of courage, an attribute which they themselves possessed in no small measure, and as they had never known injustice from Talavera and had never taken exception to his persuasions to bring them into the Christian Faith, they were ready to listen to him.

Following Talavera came Tendilla, riding among them with a small escort of his soldiers. As he took off his hat and threw it into the crowd a great cry of pleasure went up, for this was a sign that he came in peace.

The Moors were ready to listen to these two men whom they trusted.

Tendilla explained that if they persisted in their revolt they would come into conflict with the Spanish Sovereigns, and they had only to consider the power possessed by Isabella and Ferdinand to realize that they could not possibly stand against

47

them. Let them lay down their arms, let them return peacefully to their work; he would go to the Sovereigns and ask that they might be pardoned for their insurrection; and he felt sure that he would win that pardon. As a sign of his good faith he would leave his own wife and son as hostages in the Albaycin.

To this the Moors agreed, and the insurrection was over.

Some Catholic historians have sought to depict the Moors as untrustworthy barbarians because they did not believe in the Christian story. Yet Tendilla, who knew them very well indeed, could leave his wife and child as hostages. This is merely one incident which points to the integrity of the Moors. It is doubly significant that at the time when Ximenes was so flagrantly breaking the Contract of Granada, Tendilla could trust the Moorish rebels with his wife and son.

There seemed to be one desire among fanatical Christians; this was to force others to believe as they believed. How this aim was to be achieved seemed of little importance to them. This is the essence of the spirit which first established the Inquisition and caused it to flourish.

Ximenes realized that news would very quickly reach Isabella and Ferdinand in Seville of what was happening in Granada, and he was anxious that they should hear his account of the proceedings before they heard any other.

This seems to point to the fact that Ximenes at this stage of his career was very eager indeed to keep the power which had fallen into his hands. He had come a long way from the forest of Our Lady of Castañar. Perhaps he had begun to deceive himself, had begun to argue with the hermit within him: It is my duty to the Faith to remain in power that I may thus bring others to see the glory of God. However, Ximenes certainly seemed eager to keep the good opinion of Isabella and Ferdinand, to which, at the time of his appointment to the Archbishopric of Toledo he had seemed indifferent.

He therefore hastily wrote his account and sent the fleetest of his negro slaves with it to the Court at Seville. Unfortunately for Ximenes his slave lingered on the way. Perhaps certain enemies of Ximenes lured the man to a tavern and there made him drink more than was good for him and his mission. The fact was that the slave became intoxicated and, while he lingered in his drunken stupor, others reached Seville with the news.

Isabella was deeply distressed. She had been anxious that the Treaty should be observed for she wanted no trouble in Granada which had lived so peacefully since it had come under her domination. One can imagine Ferdinand's dismay secretly tinged with satisfaction. It is reputed that he was overheard saying triumphantly to the Queen: 'Ha, Señora! We are paying dear for your friend, the Archbishop! See what his rash acts are costing us! We have lost, in a matter of hours, that for which we fought over many years!'

How much better, Ferdinand implied, to have given the post to my son, a man of breeding, of royal blood, a man who would know how to carry his power and position; you must now see the folly of giving the highest post in Spain to a man of the people!

Isabella, knowing nothing of the drunken slave, could not understand why there was no news from Ximenes, and she wrote to him sternly.

When Ximenes received Isabella's letter he left at once for Seville.

There must have been great power in Ximenes. Perhaps that indifference to the good opinion of the Sovereigns (for even if it were not entirely genuine, it would seem so) convinced them of his piety.

Yes, he assured them, he and he alone was responsible for the revolt in Granda. Yes, he had acted on his own initiative without asking permission of the Sovereigns.

Perhaps the Sovereigns were reminded of that occasion when Torquemada had come to them; then Ferdinand and Isabella had been inclined to allow the Jews to remain in Spain on the payment of 30,000 ducats, but Torquemada had cried: 'Judas Iscariot sold his Master for thirty pieces of silver; you would do so for thirty thousand.'

Surely that indifference to royalty, so rarely encountered, must have given the impression of complete honesty. And as

49

with Torquemada, so with Ximenes. The King and Queen were confronted by that countenance, pallid and wasted from fasting – such undeniable evidence of the life of privation; they would have been impressed – particularly Isabella – by the obvious piety of this man. He had acted without consent, declared Ximenes, because he knew that had he asked for it, it might well have been refused.

This arrogance would seem to them sincerity, and they assured themselves that they were in the presence of a most unusual man. Thus he swayed them by his eloquence, his zeal for the faith and his seeming indifference to worldly benefits; and when he saw that the Sovereigns had become so impressed by his argument that they had ceased to blame him, he began to advise them as to the punishment which should be meted out to the Moors.

They had been guilty of treason but the Sovereigns must show mercy; let them offer the Moors baptism or exile. This was the way to create an all-Catholic Spain.

As a result of the insurrection, many of the Moors left Spain, and many more accepted baptism. Approximately 50,000 became 'Christians' at this time. They were known as *Moriscos*.

Talavera wished to have the Bible translated into Arabic that the new converts might understand the Faith into which they had been forced. Ximenes was against this; and how typical is this reasoning of him and his kind. No, said Ximenes, the Gospels were not to be given to the ignorant. The Bible should remain a mystery to them; they would have more respect for what they did not understand!

The revolt in Granada had far-reaching effects.

In the Alpujarras, that range of mountains which runs to the sea between Granada and Almería, there were many Moorish villages; the people who inhabited them lived a less civilized life than those who inhabited the towns, and were wild by nature.

News of what had happened in Granada reached them; they understood that many of their race had been forced to leave the homes which had been theirs for centuries and that many more had been forced to baptism. They anticipated that those methods of coercion, which had brought about the existing state of affairs in Granada, would soon be applied to the villages of the Alpujarras.

They therefore gathered together an army and sought to defend themselves against Christian intrusion. They tried to show their determination by attacking Christian towns.

Tendilla decided that this rebellion must be quashed before it was allowed to grow. Fortunately for him there was in Granada at that time one of the most famous of Spanish soldiers, Gonsalvo de Cordova, who was to be known as the 'Great Captain', and into this man's hands Tendilla put the task of defeating the mountain dwellers.

Gonsalvo de Cordova first turned his attention to the fortified town of Huejar; this presented great difficulty, for the Moors had dug trenches in the fields which surrounded it and, as Gonsalvo's cavalry advanced, they sank into them while the Moors from the walls of the city attacked. However, there can be no doubt of Gonsalvo's military genius, and in spite of this difficult start he had soon captured Huejar where little mercy was shown. The majority of the men were slain by the sword while the women and children were taken into slavery.

The wild men of the mountains were far from subdued by the terrible fate of Huejar. Ferdinand himself took the field against them and after some difficulty captured the town of Lanjaron, approaching it by surprise after traversing the dangerous mountains. Its inhabitants were submitted to the same treatment as those of Huejar.

After the capture of this town the Moors sued for peace, which Ferdinand granted for the surrender of their arms with certain fortresses and a payment of fifty thousand ducats. Missionaries were immediately sent into the Alpujarras villages that the conversions to Christianity might go on. Many of these people realized that there was no choice left to them and, following the example of the Moors of Granada, they submitted to baptism.

There were however some Moors who were determined to fight for their faith, and there was a further insurrection in the mountains known as the Sierra Vermeja (the Red Sierra, so called on account of the colour of the rocks) which lie between Ronda and Gibraltar. Here Alonso de Aguilar, the elder brother of Gonsalvo de Cordova, the Great Captain, went into action with his son Don Pedro de Cordova.

This family were noted for their bravery and military skill, but in this battle Don Pedro was wounded (and was carried protesting from the battlefield on his father's orders) while Alonos himself lost his life in personal conflict with the great Arab fighter, Feri de Ben Estepar.

Here also fell Francisco Ramirez, Ferdinand's great engineer whose use of gunpowder had been so effective before Granada.

The Christians were defeated, and Ferdinand led a strong body of men from Ronda, determined to avenge the fallen. The Moors however realized that their victory could only be a local one and that, ranged against them, was the whole might of Spain. They sued for peace.

Ferdinand, furious as he was by the defeat his men had suffered, passionately called out for vengeance; but Ferdinand was a shrewd ruler; he realized that further fighting could only result in loss on his side as well as that of his enemies, and he decided to grant the peace for which the Moors were asking.

He gave the Moors the now familiar choice. They could be baptized into the Christian Faith or leave the country. He himself would provide the transport they needed at the price of ten doblas of gold for each person.

Some Moors emigrated; many stayed behind and were baptized. It must have been very difficult for these people. For eight centuries Spain had been their home, and now it could be theirs no longer, unless they professed to give up the beliefs in which they and their ancestors had been brought up, and accept a Faith which was alien to them.

It is said that many more would have left the country if they could have found the money to pay for their passage.

In the year 1502, Isabella and Ferdinand issued a *pragmática* in which they declared that it was the duty of all Castilians to drive the enemies of the Faith from the land; and all Moors, who had not received baptism and who lived in the kingdoms of Castile and Léon, must leave the country; no male over the age of fourteen must stay, nor must females over the age of twelve; they were given until April to leave (the *pragmática* was published in February); they would be allowed to sell their property but, as in the case of the Jews, they might not take gold or silver out of the country!

It was apparent that the only course open to many thousands was baptism.

It was ten years since Granada had capitulated, and ten years since the signing of the treaty. Ximenes' action, in first of all so tormenting the Moors that they revolted, and then advising the breaking of the treaty as a punishment for the revolt, brings no credit to him. His conduct in this affair shows him to be as devoid of Christian charity as his prototype, Tomás de Torquemada; it was the existence of men such as these that made it possible for the Inquisition to flourish in Spain.

The *Moriscos* had appeared. Baptized as Christians they could no longer keep aloof from the Inquisition. Since its establishment in Castile under the instructions of Torquemada it had dealt severely with the *Marranos*; now here was a fresh source of victims hitherto untapped; the Inquisition was eagerly awaiting the *Moriscos*.

CHAPTER FOUR

DEZA AND LUCERO, INQUISITORS

When Torquemada died, his place as Inquisitor-General was taken by Diego de Deza. Deza was born at Toro and like Ximenes' his origins were humble. When he was young he became a Dominican and soon called attention to himself by the devout life he led and his aptitude for learning. His superiors brought him to the notice of Ferdinand and Isabella, and he was called to the Court where he was made tutor to the Infante Juan.

This naturally gave him great influence, and he eventually became Archbishop of Seville. He must have been a man of extraordinary talents to have risen so far from lowly beginnings; and in addition to other honours, Ferdinand appointed him his confessor, and the Sovereigns placed great trust in him.

It was Deza who, at the time when Columbus was seeking the help of the Sovereigns in his enterprise, threw in the weight of his influence with that of Cardinal Mendoza on the side of the adventurer, and was certainly in some part responsible for the favours shown to Columbus.

It was a pity that a man of such undoubted talents should have dissipated them in the service of the Inquisition; for, following on Torquemada, Deza undoubtedly felt that he must emulate the master, and during his term of office the cruelties of the Inquisition increased.

The bigotry of Deza is displayed in his dealings with the scholar, Elio Antonio de Nebrija.

Isabella had long realized the importance of culture to her people and she had lifted the *alcavala* (a tax of ten per cent) on all books coming into the country. Torquemada in 1490 burned hundreds of Jewish books and later, at an *auto de fé* in Salamanca, as many as six thousand Jewish volumes were sent up in flames. Ximenes acted similarly, as already mentioned, with Arabic volumes in Granada.

Anyone discovering heresy in books was in duty bound to take them, within a week of its discovery, to his bishop or the inquisitor for his district. It was stated that there was no penalty for failing to deliver such a book into the hands of authority (and here again was one of the inquisitorial quibbles), although any who failed to do so laid themselves open to violent suspicion of harbouring heretical tendencies; and such must almost certainly render examination by the Inquisitors necessary. Anyone who wrote a book tainted with heresy was, naturally, a self-confessed heretic. Any who possessed such a book was merely a suspect.

By the year 1502, Isabella and Ferdinand began to realize the enormous power of literature, and they decreed that no book should be printed in Spain or imported into that country without a licence; and before it received this it should be submitted to a thorough examination. In Ciudad Real and Valladolid the president judges of the royal courts were appointed censors; in almost every other town this duty fell to archbishops and bishops. Booksellers and printers were asked to look after the cost of these operations! If any printer or bookseller attempted to circulate a book which had not passed through the censorship, that book was confiscated and burned publicly, while the bookseller and printer concerned were no longer allowed to carry on in their business.

This was a civic law and outside the jurisdiction of the Inquisition; but the Inquisitors, greedy for power, and feeling that the censorship of books came within the range of their duties, found means of making this matter one of their concerns, for it was a fact that secular officers were less zealous in such duties than were the men of the Church.

It was thus that Deza came into conflict with Elio Antonio de Nebrija.

Ximenes was preparing his Complutensian Polyglot Bible, a work which took fifteen years to complete. It was written in four languages (Latin, Greek, Hebrew and Aramaic) and

Ximenes had engaged several collaborators to help him with the work, one of whom was the scholar, Elio Antonio de Nebrija, who, in the course of his labours, corrected certain errors in the Vulgate, that Latin version of the Bible which was, two hundred years after its completion, generally accepted in the Western Christian Church.

Deza saw a reason here to attack Nebrija whom he said was guilty of sacrilege because he dared to tamper with the Scriptures. He had, declared Deza, dared to presume that the rules of grammar were more important than the orthodox faith.

'What slavery is this!' wrote Nebrija. 'What iniquitous domination which prevents, by violence, a man from speaking as he feels, even though he does not interfere in the least with religion. It is not permitted to write even if one is alone within four walls. It is not permitted to examine and investigate for the discovery of truth, if a man allow a word to escape him.'

(*Rule & Bibliotheca Hispanica A., art. Antonius*).

Ximenes, powerful Archbishop of Toledo that he was, could not entirely save his collaborator from the fiery Deza; and Nebrija, known as one of the greatest of Spanish scholars was forced to retire from the work, although Ximenes was able to save him from greater calamity; and instead of this learned man's being wakened by night with the sound of the *alguazils* at his doorstep and dragged into the gloomy prisons of the Inquisition, he was merely required to abandon that work for which he possessed a rare skill very difficult to replace.

Ximenes must have been deeply frustrated. His Polyglot Bible, like the university of Alcalá which he founded, was a very dear project; but although he could save his friend from more violent persecution he could not bring him out of exile, where he remained until Deza was replaced in his office as Inquisitor-General by Ximenes himself. When this occurred the scholar was brought out of retirement and once more set to work on the Bible.

Ximenes is said to have begged his collaborators to lose no

time in this great work, for if he were to die they would lose their patron; and if any of them died he would be made desolate, for he valued their work more than all the riches and honours the world could bestow on him.

This incident gives a strong clue to the character of Diego de Deza, the man who replaced Torquemada at the head of the Inquisition.

One of Deza's first actions on being invested with the office of Inquisitor-General was directed against certain Jews who, homesick for the country in which they and their ancestors had lived, returned after the great exodus of 1492. The Jews pretended to be newcomers to the country and when they were arrested declared that their great desire was to embrace the Christian Faith.

The new Inquisitor-General took stern action against them and an Edict was issued which declared that all Jews and Jewesses who entered Spain should be punished by death, and that their property should pass to the state.

There must be no failure to carry out the strict laws against them; only those Jews who, before entering the country had already made known their desire to return and be converted and who went before a notary with witnesses and publicly became Christians, would be allowed to stay. If any came into the country and failed to carry out these instructions they must immediately suffer confiscation of their property and death.

In spite of all the suffering which members of their race had endured, some Jews did return to Spain, notwithstanding the fact that by becoming New Christians they placed themselves within the grasp of the Inquisition.

In the year 1500 Deza produced a Constitution in seven articles. These were:

1. There should be examination of every town and village in which the Inquisition had not yet been set up.
2. All persons should be reminded yet again in no uncertain terms of their duty to pass on to the authorities any information they might discover concerning the suspicious conduct of family, friends and acquaintances.

3. There should be a search for books, and all persons mentioned in such a way as to place them under suspicion should be arrested.

4. Those who committed blasphemy and such minor sins should not be brought before the Inquisition, for these were not worthy of its attention which should be directed with greater force against heretics.

5. When a person had been vindicated it should be necessary for two witnesses to swear responsibility for the vindicated person's orthodoxy.

6. Those who had been vehemently suspected, and abjured, should swear solemnly to have no more communication with heretics but to inform against them.

7. Those who abjured after conviction of heresy should also swear to have no more intercourse with heretics and to inform against them.

Although there was nothing very new in these seven articles this was a sign that Diego de Deza intended to get to work with vigour and there followed Deza's election a reign of terror which exceeded even that endured under Torquemada; and this reached its zenith in Cordova where the most venomously cruel of Inquisitors, Lucero, was established.

Diego Rodríguez Lucero was given the name of Tenebrero – agent of darkness – and he soon had the whole of Cordova reduced to a state of terror.

He was a man who was already in high favour with the Sovereigns who had bestowed upon him a canonry in Cadiz; and the number of heretics whom he brought to judgment was so large that both Isabella and Ferdinand complimented him upon this. They were grateful for the large sums which were flowing into the treasury through the work of this man.

Lucero had no compunction in the methods he used. Torture was liberally applied to the prisoners for the sole purpose of incriminating more and more people. Lucero's great desire was to have the prisons of Cordova overflowing, while the possessions of these unfortunate people were taken from them to swell the treasury of the Inquisition and State and win for the

Inquisitor of Cordova the thanks of his grateful Sovereigns.

A letter in the Achivo de Simancas tells how two men, Alfonso Fernández Herrero and Fernando de Cordova escaped from the purge and sought refuge in Portugal. Without asking royal permission to do so, Lucero immediately despatched *alguazils* to bring them back.

This was against international law and Emanuel was naturally furious at the high-handed conduct of the Inquisitor. He refused to relinquish the two men who had sought refuge in his country unless he was given a detailed account of their sins.

Lucero, assured of his Sovereigns' support, immediately appealed to them with the result that Emanuel was asked out of the affection he bore Isabella and Ferdinand to give up the two wanted men. He was gently reminded that he must lay no impediment in the path of the Holy Office and that by doing so he was working against the glory of God.

The people of Cordova were naturally deeply disturbed to have such a man in such a position in their city. And not only were the ordinary citizens disturbed; the authorities were also growing uneasy. There is an account of a clash between the mayor of Cordova and Lucero. The mayor showed his contempt for Lucero and the Inquisition in a public square of the town during an auction of confiscated property. The mayor was hastily removed and put into prison. The sentence which was passed on him was a harsh one. He was dismissed from his office for life and was not to fulfil any other public position. He was to be banished from Cordova, which he must prepare to leave in a week.

Thus Lucero showed the people of Cordova what happened to those who sought to flout him.

Complimented by the Sovereigns on his zeal, Lucero became more and more zealous. More arrests were made without reason and many noblemen and even good churchmen – if they happened to be Old Christians – were hustled into jail. The machines of torture were working constantly. Lucero was eager to incriminate as many people of wealth as possible; no one knew in what direction the next attack would be made. There were stories of plots to establish Judaism in Cordova and over-

59

throw the Catholic Church throughout the land. No man, woman or child in the city of Cordova was safe.

This was a state of affairs which could not be tolerated.

Meanwhile events of historical importance had been taking place in Spain.

Isabella was drawing very near to the end of her life. The calamitous misfortunes of her family had given her great cause for anxiety; and these misfortunes undoubtedly hastened her end.

The Infante Juan was dead, and he died without giving Spain an heir; her beloved daughter Isabella, Queen of Portugal, had quickly followed him; but perhaps the greatest misfortune of all was the growing insanity of her daughter Juana, who was now heir to the throne of Castile.

Juana's strange conduct was causing comment wherever she went; and this was worsened by the fact that her husband known as Philip the Handsome, was notoriously unfaithful to Juana who doted on him and was given to frantic displays of jealousy.

Accounts of these outbursts must have brought humiliation to Isabella; particularly as, after one of them, Philip had declared his intention of never again having intercourse with his wife. This was an occasion when the fickle Philip became enamoured of one of Juana's ladies and, according to his custom, made no secret of his preference. This particular young woman was noted for her beautiful golden hair which Philip particularly admired.

Juana, driven into one of her mad rages by her jealousy, had the woman brought to her, bound her hand and foot and caused her hair to be sheared.

When Philip saw what had happened he announced his intention to cut himself off from his wife.

The effect of such scandal on the pious Isabella can well be imagined. It was fortunate however that Philip and Juana already had two sons, both born before she showed signs of insanity. One of these was Charles, born on 24th February, 1500, and to achieve great fame as the Emperor Charles V of

Austria, and I of Spain; and the other was Ferdinand, born on the 10th March in 1503.

Those last months of Isabella's life must have been indeed uneasy when she contemplated the crown which she must leave behind, and thought of her ambitious husband and son-in-law, her grandsons – one in his cradle, the other only just out of it – and her poor mad daughter Juana the heiress of Castile.

In the midst of all this trouble Ferdinand caught a fever and Isabella was very anxious on her husband's behalf. This anxiety, coupled with her melancholy over her daughter Juana, weakened Isabella considerably and she became very depressed over Ferdinand's illness and refused to believe the doctors when they assured her that the illness was far from fatal and that Ferdinand would recover.

Ferdinand did recover, but Isabella herself had contracted the fever and, in her case, there was less resilience to fight against it.

Her condition grew weaker and it became apparent to all about the Court – including Isabella herself – that she was near to death.

She was always conscious of her duties and received ambassadors whilst being unable to rise from her bed; and she continued to conduct state business, sick as she was.

In October of that year 1504 she began to prepare that elaborate and revealing document: her will.

In this she asked that her body be taken to the Franciscan monastery of Santa Isabella in the Alhambra and there buried with the utmost simplicity; but should Ferdinand on his death prefer a more elaborate tomb in a different spot, then her body should be taken from its humble resting place and laid beside that of her husband. This was to be a sign that in life they had been united, and in death were not divided.

She then went on to donate certain sums to charity and to arrange that all her debts should be discharged within a year; she stressed to her successors the importance of maintaining the integrity of the kingdom and retaining control of Gibraltar.

The crown of Castile she settled on her daughter Juana – as

Queen Proprietor – and on Juana's husband, Archduke Philip, together with much advice.

She then wrote of the government of the realm in the absence of Juana or at such other times as she should be incapable of ruling. She therefore appointed her husband Ferdinand as Regent until the time when her grandson Charles should be of an age to rule.

There were other bequests, and the two main executors were Ferdinand and Ximenes.

On the 26th of November 1504, only three days after the execution of her will, she died.

Ferdinand resigned the crown of Castile and in the great square at Toledo the new rulers were proclaimed. Juana and Philip were at this time in Flanders and, in accordance with the terms of Isabella's will, Ferdinand took up the regency.

The Castilians however were not pleased to see an Aragonese ruling over them even as Regent. They had accepted Ferdinand during the life of Isabella because they had looked upon him merely as the husband of their Queen; it was a different matter when he was ruling without her. Certain lords, among them Juan Pacheco, Marquis of Villena, and the Duke of Najara, corresponded with Archduke Philip and persuaded him to demand complete supremacy in Castile and that Ferdinand should retire to Aragon.

Ferdinand's reply to this was a contemptuous refusal and a demand to know how Philip thought he could govern a people like the Spaniards when he knew so little of them. Ferdinand did however advise him that it would be advantageous if he and Juana came to Castile to show themselves to the people.

Meanwhile Ferdinand's enemies grew in number. Philip, it was understood, was generous, and Ferdinand's parsimonious ways had been long deplored.

Juana, who was being treated badly by her husband, wrote a letter in which she stated her belief that her father should be allowed to continue to rule Castile. The secretary to whom Juana had entrusted this letter was betrayed and sent to a dungeon. Philip, furious with his wife, put her under guard and kept her a prisoner in conditions which increased her wildness.

To add to his troubles Ferdinand discovered that Philip, with the help of his father, the Emperor Maximilian, was attempting to win the confidence of Gonsalvo de Cordova, the great Captain who was in command of Naples, with a view to annexing Naples as a dependency of Castile. Ferdinand had always been shrewd and he now saw that the only way of combating the claims of Philip and Maximilian was to win the French to his side; Louis XII, who had his eyes on Naples, had been delighted by the conflict between Ferdinand and his son-in-law; he was however a little disturbed to contemplate the enormous inheritance which would eventually come to Philip. It seemed that not only would Castile but the whole of Spain eventually fall into his hands, with Austria, Flanders and Burgundy, in addition to those rich lands which, since the discovery of America, had become appendages of Spain.

Ferdinand was fully aware of this, and he decided to take that step which never failed to bring two countries closer together. It was but a short time since the death of Isabella, but Ferdinand was ready to contemplate a French marriage.

Accordingly it was decided that he should marry Germaine de Foix, who was the daughter of a sister of Louis XII; her grandmother was that Leonora who had poisoned her sister Blanche for the throne of Navarre (see *The Rise of the Spanish Inquisition*).

To Germaine Louis resigned his claims to Naples, and it was part of her dowry that these should be secured to her and her heirs. A treaty of alliance and commerce was made between the two sovereigns, and Ferdinand was to pay one million gold ducats in ten yearly instalments to defray the expenses Louis had incurred during the Neapolitan war. (Prescott's *History of the Reign of Ferdinand and Isabella*). Ferdinand came badly out of the agreement; he must have missed the sound good sense of Isabella and he was no doubt disconcerted to feel that he must seek help from France against his own son-in-law.

Now that Ferdinand had a powerful ally in his father-in-law, Philip appeared to be a little more accommodating. In the Concord of Salamanca, which was signed on 24th November, 1505, it was agreed that Castile should be governed in the names of Ferdinand, Philip and Juana, but that Ferdinand should have one half of the revenues.

Ferdinand could congratulate himself that his new alliance had given Philip reason to pause and consider before continuing his high-handed policy; but on the 8th January, 1506, Philip left Zealand intending to visit Spain.

Storm drove him to England where he and Juana were received in great friendliness by Henry VII. They were taken to Windsor where they were entertained for three months. They returned to Spain on the 28th April, only six weeks after the marriage of Ferdinand and Germaine had taken place.

Arriving in Spain Philip had with him three thousand German soldiers; and a larger number of Spaniards hastened to place themselves under his command. Philip then announced that he was no longer agreeable to the Concord of Salamanca and was determined that he and his wife alone should rule Castile.

Ferdinand was now to realize to the full the power which he had enjoyed through Isabella. The French marriage had not endeared him even to those who supported his claims; and the diplomatic skill of Ximenes could gain nothing for Ferdinand's cause.

At length it was decided that Ferdinand and Philip should meet in a field near Puebla de Senabria on the boundary of Léon and Galicia.

Philip came surrounded by his soldiers, archers and light cavalry, making a glittering display. Ferdinand came attended only by two hundred gentlemen who were weaponless.

The two kings dismounted and went to a house attended only by their most trusted advisers: Philip knew how strong his position was; and Ferdinand was forced to agree that Juana and Philip should be the sole sovereigns of Castile; he also agreed that his daughter was incapable of ruling, and made a declaration that he would help Philip in every way in the government of Castile, although he stated that he made these concessions under protest and solely to prevent civil war; he would continue to consider his claims to the regency valid and he would, as soon as he was in a position to do so, seek to bring Juana from the captivity which her husband had imposed upon her.

Ferdinand returned to Aragon, and Philip went to Valladolid to receive the homage due to him as ruler of Castile. It was necessary to bring Juana from her captivity that she might appear with him; and this he did, though much against his will. Juana accompanied him dressed in garments of mourning; and at Valladolid they received the oath of allegiance to Juana as Queen, to Philip as her consort, and to their elder son, young Charles, who was recognized as Juana's heir.

Philip now took control; all the high places at his Court went to the Flemish; if the people had had cause to complain of Ferdinand's parsimonious ways they now had greater cause to regret Philip's extravagance.

Ximenes, in his position as Primate of Spain, remonstrated with Philip, who at this stage dared show nothing but respect for this important man, but quite clearly he was seeking ways of escaping from his influence.

Meanwhile the people were disturbed not only by Philips' extravagance and his lechery, but by the humiliating position into which he had forced his wife who was the true Queen of Castile.

It was at this time that events in Cordova, which was suffering from the Inquisitor Lucero, came to a head.

Many members of the prominent families of Cordova had been arrested and were imprisoned in the dungeons of the Inquisition; others had been brought before the tribunal for listening to the preacher Membreque, and over one hundred of them were burned alive.

Lucero was even worse than his predecessor, Doctor Guiral, Dean of Guadix, who had been sent from Cordova to Avila in 1499. He had been suspected of nefarious practices and at length the Inquisitor-General had had to take action against him. His case – as that of Lucero – is very interesting because it gives an indication of what was happening behind the carefully guarded walls of the Inquisition, and consequently a light is shone into places which Inquisitors had been at such pains to keep in darkness.

It was discovered that Guiral had made as much as 150,000 *maravedis* by selling 'exemptions' to victims. This meant that on payment of a certain sum, arranged between them, to the dishonest Inquisitor, a man or woman who had been sentenced to wear the *sanbenito*, was excused from doing so. Guiral had not kept his hands off confiscated property, and in this way, among other treasures he was the possessor of ninety-three very valuable pearls. He imposed fines on all whom he accused of withholding confiscated property and was not too proud to collect a few ducats from his humblest servants. He entered into negotiations with *Conversos* accepting large sums in exchange for allowing them to evade confiscation of the whole of their property. This business man was eventually arrested and brought to trial (Archivo de Simancas). The result of his trial is not known, but his misdeeds could not have been taken very seriously to heart because when Lucero took his place he behaved with equal dishonesty and much more cruelty.

Perhaps he was allowed to continue unmolested because although he looked after his own interests he was not blind to those of his masters, and during his term of office treasure flowed into the coffers of the Inquisition and the State.

One of his accomplices – very wisely chosen by Lucero – was Juan Róiz de Calcena, who, for inquisitorial purposes, was Ferdinand's secretary. He took his cut of the profits and made sure that excellent accounts of Inquisitor Lucero of Cordova reached the ears of Ferdinand.

In 1507 the Captain Gonzalo de Avora wrote a letter to the royal secretary Almazan in which he discusses the methods of the Inquisition. He says that these methods were such that they defamed the kingdom and destroyed without justice a great part of it, slaying and robbing, violating maidens and wives – and all this brought great dishonour to the Christian religion (Lea).

However, Ferdinand stood firmly behind Lucero because Lucero's accomplice was Calcena, who was always at hand to give Ferdinand a good account of his friend.

Lucero had in one of his prisons a man named Diego de Algiciras. Lucero only had to imply that he wanted evidence against such and such a *converso* and Diego de Algiciras would willingly give what was asked. So useful was this man that he was often borrowed by the tribunal of Jaen to help them out when they needed to bring about arrests of the wealthy.

Torture was, of course, freely applied to obtain the required evidence, but it was useful to have a man on hand, eager and willing to supply it, and for five years Lucero made use of this man's services. Many unsavoury details came to light at this time, such as imprisoning a young girl of fifteen, stripping her and whipping her until she was ready to inform against her mother. There is no doubt that with such men as Lucero at its head the affairs of the Inquisition were at their most despicable.

The apprehensive people of Cordova appealed to Deza to make an enquiry into Lucero's methods of conducting the Inquisition, but Deza was evasive. The people realized that it was useless to try to put their case before Ferdinand because Calcena would either not allow any such appeal to reach him or would poison his mind in advance against those who complained. But there were Philip and Juana who might be more ready to listen. Philip was antagonistic towards the Inquisition; he had accepted bribes from the *Conversos* and the hopes of the people of Cordova were high. It seemed that he was prepared to give them justice, in which case there would certainly be an enquiry into the behaviour of Lucero.

Lucero, perhaps to make a diversion, then produced allegations against Talavera, Isabella's favourite whom she had made Archbishop of Granada. Lucero would not have dared do this while Isabella lived; but now he reminded the people that Talavera had a Jewish taint in his blood.

Talavera had a great reputation for sanctity; he had given generously to charity during his life and had few possessions of his own; he was beloved by the people, particularly the Moors of Granada who had learned to trust him.

It seemed incredible that such a pious man could have been accused of Judaizing; but naturally Lucero had his own methods of finding witnesses. He had one – a Jewish woman who had declared she was a prophetess – who had already suffered acutely under torture and it was only necessary to threaten her with more unless she supplied the required evidence against Talavera for her to say exactly what was required. Talavera's nephew, his nieces, his sisters and his servants were all arrested, but before Talavera himself could be taken up it was necessary to get permission from the Pope to do so; this was sent for.

Before it arrived, Juana and Philip had returned to Spain, and the hopes of the *Conversos* were raised once more. Ferdinand left for Naples and Philip, having locked up his wife on account of her insanity, set about ruling the land. So it now seemed possible to bring Lucero to justice. An enquiry was to be made and the wicked and wily Inquisitor, terrified of what might come to light, hastily arranged that all his prisoners should immediately be hustled to an *auto de fé* where they should perish at the stake. Orders from Philip came in time to prevent this.

Unfortunately for the suffering people of Spain at this juncture Philip was taken suddenly ill; it is said that he caught cold after playing a strenuous ball game; he developed a fever, and six days after he first became ill he died.

There are various versions of the cause of his death. His physicians are blamed for being unskilful and neglecting to bleed him in time. The many draughts of cold water which he is said to have drunk when he was overheated from his game are blamed. There were, of course, the usual suggestions that he was poisoned; and according to Bergenroth it was generally accepted at the time that this was the true cause of his death and that Ferdinand's envoy to Philip was the murderer. Ferdinand would certainly have had a motive for removing his troublesome son-in-law.

One of the physicians, who was present at the death, Dr Parra, wrote to Ferdinand that after playing this violent ball game for several hours Philip had cooled himself off too suddenly and thus caught a chill. This was followed by fever and the spitting of blood. Cupping glasses and purgatives were administered, and when he was bled the blood was 'thick and bad'. Philip grew very weak, found it difficult to speak, and then fell into unconsciousness. He was afflicted with sweating which brought out black spots on his body.

Prescott takes the view that, since Parra wrote such a letter to Ferdinand, and in view of the symptoms he described, this points to a natural death.

Yet Philip was a healthy twenty-eight, and it seems strange that a man so young should have died merely because he became overheated in a ball game and drank cold water afterwards, particularly when there were those who would find the world so much more tolerable without him.

With the death of Philip, Deza, the Inquisitor-General, immediately stepped back into office and restored Lucero to his.

The latter determined to make up for lost time by letting loose his wrath on all those who had endeavoured to put an end to his career, and the terror in Cordova was intensified. His accusations were more reckless than ever; the prisons were again full to overflowing.

But such a state of affairs could not continue. Two of the nobles of the city, the Marquis of Priego and the Count of Cabra, were ready to help the people to revolt. Priego, was particularly eager because he knew that Lucero was about to arrest him. Complaints were laid before Padre Fray Franciso de Cuesta of the Convent of La Merced who declared that Lucero was guilty and should be arrested and his property should be confiscated.

The people assembled to make the arrest. They forced their way into the alcázar which was the headquarters of the Inquisition, set the prisoners free, but looked in vain for Lucero who, having heard that they were on the way, had taken refuge in flight.

Deza, however, immediately gave an order that all those who had revolted in Cordova against the rule of Lucero should be prosecuted, and sent his nephew Pedro Juárez de Deza to carry out this order.

Lucero resumed full command and those prisoners who had been freed – including Talavera and his family – were once more arrested.

As for Talavera, by the time the testimony against him was admitted to be false, he had suffered so much from the rigours of imprisonment and anxieties on account of his family, that he did not live to enjoy his freedom.

Ferdinand was now ruling as Regent – his daughter being too unstable to wear the crown, and his grandson Charles too young – and with Ximenes at his elbow, he was forced to the decision that he must take action against the demoniacal inquisitors who seemed to want to outdo Torquemada in their cruelty.

There are some who hint that Ximenes had his eyes on Deza's position, and this may have been so since he became Inquisitor-General after Deza vacated the office, but Ximenes was a just man who would deplore the shame men like Deza and Lucero were bringing to the Holy Office.

Deza was asked to resign; but Lucero could not be allowed to escape so gracefully. His sins had been too flagrant.

He was to stand for trial, accused of forcing people to give false testimony against others. Julius II appointed an apostolic judge to try the case and on 17th October, 1507, it was decreed that Lucero should be put into prison.

Nothing however was done; and Peter Martyr, who was recording at the time and on whom we rely for this information, declares that the Supreme Council were in league with Lucero, and that the usual examination of documents and witnesses, calculated to last for a very long time, took place.

At length Lucero was arrested and taken in chains to Burgos. There Ximenes gathered together a committee headed by himself to try the case.

Ximenes, for all his harshness, was determined to be just, and hundreds of those who had been imprisoned by Lucero were set free, for it was proved that many of the accusations brought against them were groundless. Lucero was found guilty of injustice and harshness, but he was not punished on account of the thousands whom he had condemned to the stake and who had suffered the fiery death at his orders. He was merely required to retire from his post and live at Almería where he continued with his duties as *maestrescuela*, a teacher of the clergy. (Rule).

Llorente states that during Deza's term of office 2,592 people were burned alive, 896 burnt in effigy, and 34,952 were imprisoned and lost all their worldly goods.

These figures can only be approximate; and it is possible that a proportion of the 2,592 were strangled as the fires were lighted, so that they may not have been burned alive. All the same, these numbers are very shocking when it is considered that Deza's reign of office extended only from Torquemada's death in 1498 to 1507.

But the rising in Cordova had shown the rulers both in Spain and in Rome that the Inquisition was in danger if men such as Deza and Lucero were put at its head.

Ferdinand therefore nominated a new Inquisitor-General for Castile, and the Pope, Julius II, confirmed this appointment.

As a result Ximenes became Inquisitor-General of Castile, and at this time Ferdinand secured from Julius a Cardinal's hat for his minister.

Ximenes, Cardinal and Primate of Spain and Inquisitor-General of Castile, had reached the zenith of power, for he had climbed as high as it was possible for any man to climb in the Catholic Church of Spain.

He had come a long way from the hermit's hut in the forest about Our Lady of Castañar.

CHAPTER FIVE

XIMENES – INQUISITOR-GENERAL

No sooner had Ximenes taken his place as head of the Inquisition than he felt less enthusiastic concerning those reforms which previously he had felt to be necessary. He burned with zeal; he was as eager for an all-Catholic Spain as Torquemada had been; and realizing immediately that the Inquisition could be used in the service of the State, his plan was not to diminish its powers but to increase them.

As Cardinal of Spain – an honour rarely bestowed – he was second only to the Pope in the Roman Catholic Church. Politically he was second to his King; and now that he had been nominated Inquisitor-General of Castile, the administration of the Inquisition was largely in his hands.

He divided Castile into ten sections for the purposes of the Inquisition, and at the head of each section he set an Inquisitor of his choice.

In spite of his severity, he did attempt to be just, and he did aim to set right a great many anomalies which had crept into the Inquisition under the rule of Deza and Lucero.

One of the projects near to the heart of Ximenes, and ranking perhaps with that of the founding of the University of Alcalá and the compiling of the Polyglot Bible, was the desire to capture the Holy Land for Christianity and banish the Infidel from its soil.

He had, before the death of Philip, endeavoured to make an alliance between Spain, England and Portugal. These three countries were bound together by family ties, for Emanuel of Portugal was the husband of Maria, the third daughter of Isabella and Ferdinand (she had married Emanuel after the death of his first wife, her sister Isabella who had died in childbirth). England was bound to Spain by the marriage of Catalina, the youngest daughter of Isabella and Ferdinand, with Arthur Prince of Wales; in 1509, after Arthur's death, she was to marry his brother Henry VIII.

Ximenes believed that these three countries jointly could undertake a glorious campaign in the Holy Land; however the uncertainty of Ferdinand's position, the death of Philip and the insanity of Juana obliged him to shelve this project.

Ferdinand had been urged to show himself to his subjects in Naples and had in September 1506 set out on the voyage. He had been made anxious concerning his viceroy in Naples, Gonsalvo de Cordova, the Great Captain and brilliant soldier who had aroused the envy of many who sought to discredit him with his sovereign. It was during Ferdinand's journey that news reached him of the death of his son-in-law Philip. Ferdinand absent, Philip dead, and Juana mad! Here was a situation which might have caused grave disorder through the land had not the primacy been in the capable hands of Ximenes.

With admirable energy and foresight on the day before Philip's death (when it was obvious that the young man might not live) Ximenes called together a council, with himself at the head, which was to form a regency until Ferdinand's return.

There were seven members of the council: the Duke of Infantado, the Duke of Nájara (both of whom had opposed Ferdinand), the Grand Constable and the Admiral of Castile (both of whom stood firmly behind the King) and two Flemish lords. By his choice of council (with himself at its head) Ximenes displayed his determination to be just; and in this he also showed his wisdom, for the country was in a ferment and it was largely due to the skilful handling of matters by the Primate that revolution was avoided at this juncture. Ferdinand must have been once more reminded of Isabella's wisdom when she had insisted on bestowing the Archbishopric of Toledo on a man who had no great family connections to make demands upon him and was well known for his honesty of purpose (misguided though it might sometimes be).

Ferdinand did not immediately return. He was shrewd enough to understand that his presence in Castile might not have a soothing effect on a situation full of dangers; moreover he could fully trust Ximenes.

Meanwhile Henry VII of England was looking for a wife. He had hoped for Margaret, who was the widow of the young Infante Juan, son of Isabella and Ferdinand, and negotiations for their marriage were about to be brought to a conclusion when Margaret declared that in no circumstances would she marry the old King of England. Henry then turned his eyes to Spain. Juana, mad as she was, was Queen of Castile, and Henry was eager to cement the alliance with Spain.

He therefore let it be known through his daughter-in-law Catalina, that when Juana and Philip had been shipwrecked and forced to land in England he had fallen in love with Juana. There was, of course, only one thing with which Henry was capable of falling in love: wealth. He was very eager for this match.

Catalina was also eager for the marriage. She must have felt very unhappy in England; her husband was dead and her position uncertain; so that the thought of having her own sister living as Queen in the same country must have been very comforting.

Ferdinand himself wrote that, although he did not know whether his daughter would be willing to marry, he would sooner see her married to Henry VII of England than to any other prince in Christendom; he adds however: 'more particularly on the terms of the treaty which the King of England is willing to sign with me'.

In Ferdinand and Henry were to be found two of the most parsimonious of monarchs, so there was no doubt that had the terms been advantageous enough for both, they would have done all in their power to bring about the match.

To Ferdinand such a marriage seemed infinitely desirable. It would mean that Juana would go to England and while she was there he would remain Regent of Castile until his grandson Charles was old enough to rule; and as Charles was not yet seven years old, that would be a very long time.

The English, he was assured, were willing that he should remain Regent of Castile. As for the madness of Juana, the

English could not see that that should provide a deterrent to the marriage, for it was clear that whatever Juana's mental state happened to be she was capable of bearing children.

While all these suggestions for her remarriage were in progress Juana was giving more definite signs of madness. In spite of the fact that Philip had treated her as badly as he possibly could – first by his infidelity and then by imprisoning her – she had been deeply enamoured of him. It is often suggested that it was due to her possessive absorption with her handsome husband that Juana's unbalanced mind toppled over into insanity.

Dr Parra reported that during Philip's last illness Juana was constantly at his bedside and herself took charge of the nursing. However, when he died she gave way to her grief to such an extent and in such an eccentric manner that any who had previously doubted that she was insane no longer did so.

She did not weep, but shut herself into a dark room and sat as though she were a statue, her head resting on her hand; she appeared to be in a coma.

She had had the body of her husband embalmed and the coffin was taken wherever she went; each night it was set up in a position so that she could see it from her window, and she would sit staring at it, never shedding a tear; it is said that she did not shed a tear after she discovered Philip's intrigue with the Flemish woman whose hair she cut off.

At the end of the year she decided to bury Philip in Granada. The coffin was placed on a carriage of great magnificence which was drawn by four horses, and a procession in which were nobles and men of the Church left Burgos on the 20th December on the way to Granada. They were forced to travel by night, for Juana declared that she as a widow, 'the sun of whose soul had been extinguished', should never expose herself to the light of day. At every halting-place the coffin was taken to a church or a monastery where it remained throughout the day, and where a funeral service was held as though Philip had just died. Juana set a bodyguard about the coffin, her aim being to protect it from women. She continued to be jealous of women; and on one occasion, when the coffin was placed in a nunnery, she was furious because she had thought the place was a mon-

75

astery. Even when he was dead she would not allow Philip to be surrounded by women, so she ordered that the coffin be removed at once. It was taken from the grounds of the nunnery to a field some distance away. Juana's madness, which had been so aggravated by her passionate jealousy of Philip the Handsome, must have been very obvious to her companions on that night, for she insisted that the coffin be unsealed that she might examine the relics and touch them. She had to assure herself that those women at the nunnery had not sought to rob her of any part of him.

She and her party encamped in the field with the coffin; it must have been a wild and macabre scene with the mad Queen urging her servants to open the coffin by the light of torches which were continually extinguished by the howling wind.

Yet Juana had her lucid moments. Before embarking on the journey with her husband's remains she had snapped her fingers at all Philip's favourites who had profited so much since they came with him to Spain. She revoked all grants made since the death of her mother; and she stubbornly refused to recall her father.

Mad as she was, she seemed to understand at times that she was the Queen.

She continued however on the grim journey to Granada, wearing clothes that were dark, dirty and tattered; and when Ferdinand returned to Spain in August 1507 she, in the company of Ximenes met him at Tortoles.

Ferdinand was horrified at the sight of his daughter for he scarcely recognized her in her wild state; but he persuaded her to give up her travelling by night from place to place in that melancholy cortège; and as a result she went to the Castle of Tordesillas taking the coffin with her. Philip was later buried in the monastery of Santa Clara which adjoined the palace of Tordesillas; thus Juana could from her window look on the tomb of her husband.

Juana, Queen of Castile in name only, remained in the palace for forty-seven years never leaving it.

The remains of Philip were eventually removed to Granada

and placed in the Cathedral Church; Juana was placed beside her husband and a sepulchre was built for them by their son Charles V near that of Ferdinand and Isabella.

Juana's madness has been the subject of some controversy. Bergenroth brings forward an interesting theory, and Bergenroth is a writer who made such intensive researches into the history of Spain that his theories are well worth consideration. He was born in 1813, son of a Prussian magistrate, and in his youth was appointed to the post of assessor to the court of Cologne; he also worked in other German towns. Being involved in revolutionary movements he found it necessary to leave this native land, and went to California—a very different place in those days of the 1850's from what it is today. He became head of a gang of adventurers, narrowly escaped death, and continued to live dangerously until he suddenly became homesick for Europe.

He returned to Europe to write historical works – first in London and then in Spain. He went to Simancas, a Castilian village not far from Valladolid where he knew there was an enormous source of hitherto untapped information, for the archives had been kept in this village since the time of Philip II.

He stayed there for eight years and eventually died of typhus, which he had no hope of evading in the squalid little village. But during his stay there he selected documents, collected them, deciphered them, and eventually edited three volumes of the Calendar of State Papers.

Bergenroth states that the story of Juana's madness must be discarded. He believed that she was sane until the very end of her life when, after so many years of imprisonment, her reason deserted her, as might happen to most people who had been subjected to such treatment. She was kept a prisoner, says Bergenroth, for the benefit of the three rulers of Spain: Ferdinand, Philip and Charles.

Ferdinand was eager to make it known that she was insane so that he might rule as Regent; he did not wish her to die, but merely to be out of the way, for her death could avail him nothing. If she died her son Charles would be the King of Castile, and Ferdinand's position would be no better.

As for Philip, if Juana had died he would have had no claim whatsoever to the throne of Castile; it was therefore to his interest to keep her alive but powerless. How could he be better served than by her 'madness'?

It was in the interest of these two ambitious men that she should continue to live, while being judged unable to rule.

Charles, says Herr Bergenroth, wished his mother to be out of the way that he might reign alone, so it was to his advantage to support the theory of madness.

Prescott, discussing this theory of Bergenroth, finds it 'ludicrous', and he points out that had she died Ferdinand's position would not have changed; he could still have hoped for the regency until Charles was of age. Philip had he lived also might have ruled in the place of his son until Charles grew up.

Bergenroth does not seem to have taken into consideration the fact that Juana was mad at times and sane at others; and that there were occasions when, had Juana wished, she could have asserted her rights yet did not do so.

On considering all the available evidence there seems to be very little doubt that Juana was indeed periodically mad and that Ferdinand, Philip and Charles must be exonerated from the charge of imprisoning Juana merely for their own advantage.

Since the Moors had been driven from Spain there had been frequent raids on the coast by Moorish pirates who had set up their headquarters in various ports on the north coast of Africa. One of these ports was Mazalquivir, a mere two or three miles from Oran, almost opposite Carthagena.

Ximenes who, during the uncertainty in Castile, had been forced to abandon his grandiose schemes for the capture of the Holy Land, was determined to make a start on his grand project. If he could take Mazalquivir, Oran would be his next objective, and Oran was a considerable port, the chief market for the trade of the Levant with a population of some twenty thousand. Its capture would, Ximenes was sure, strike a strong blow for Christendom.

Ximenes approached Ferdinand, pointing out the advantages

to Spain of the capture of Mazalquivir. Ferdinand agreed on this but he regretted he had no money for the enterprise, whereupon Ximenes offered to provide funds from his own revenues.

Ximenes was prepared to find this, for he had made up his mind that Mazalquivir was to be the first step in the capture of the Holy Land; so preparations were made – Ferdinand being eager to suppress Moorish piracy, Ximenes eager to suppress the Infidel or to make Christians of them.

The expedition was successful and, after a hard struggle which lasted for fifty days, the port was captured for Christian Spain. This was on 13th September, 1505.

Ximenes was delighted, but it was at this point that internal affairs in Spain began to be so complicated and dangerous, that further plans for extending Christianity had to be postponed.

Later however, in 1509, when Ximenes had become a Cardinal and Grand-Inquisitor, he was eager to continue with his conquests, and his objective was the important town of Oran.

Ximenes knew that he would be expected to finance this expedition, as he had the previous one, and was prepared to advance the money. This he did; he must have been a very rich man, for the building of the University of Alcalá was a continual strain on his resources yet he did not suspend this. The project was reviewed with great interest throughout Castile; not because a man of the Church had appeared to become a Generalissimo of the armies (previous Archbishops of Toledo, Mendoza and Carillo, had ridden into battle) but because many believed they saw in it a state of friction between Ferdinand and Ximenes. Ximenes was a man of the utmost importance; he had actually been Regent during the absence of Ferdinand; and Ferdinand, aware as he was of the brilliance of Ximenes, could never forget that he had been chosen by Isabella to fill a post which Ferdinand had greatly desired for his own bastard son.

It was now that Ximenes' motive in the Oran adventure was to get Ferdinand out of the country so that he might again occupy the position of Regent.

Whether Ferdinand himself believed this, we do not know, but it is suggested that he put forward the idea that Ximenes should lead the expedition. Yet it appears to be a fact that Ximenes had determined from the first to lead the expedition himself.

Ximenes must have aroused an irritation in Ferdinand, perhaps because he was Archbishop of Toledo, perhaps because of that self-righteousness of Ximenes, a very irritating quality to a man of Ferdinand's nature who, while he declared himself to be a firm adherent of the Catholic Church, had been guilty of many sins which would be shocking to a man such as Ximenes. However, from the beginning it seems that Ferdinand – although he would derive great advantages from the success of the expedition – was determined to put obstacles in its way.

For instance, the expedition needed a military leader who must be the finest soldier available, and there was one who was ideal for the post. This was Gonsalvo de Cordova, the Great Captain. Ximenes wished this man to take command, but Ferdinand, who had doubted the Captain's loyalty during his vice-regency in Naples, refused to allow the Great Captain to lead the expedition, and threatened to cancel it unless another man was chosen.

So in place of the Great Captain, Ximenes was obliged to take Count Pedro Navarro, a choice which was to prove to be a bad one from his point of view.

Many of the nobles then became sceptical of the whole affair and asked each other what success could come of a project when a monk set out to fight the battles of Spain and the greatest soldier in the country was left at home to count his beads like a hermit.

It was on the 16th of May, 1509, that the Fleet set out for Mazalquivir. When they landed, Ximenes on his mule rode along beside the soldiers, a friar in the Franciscan costume riding before him, carrying the huge silver cross.

Trouble broke out between Ximenes and Navarro before the battle. Navarro wished the troops to rest before going into action, but Ximenes answered that the battle was to be one between Jesus Christ and the false prophet Mohammed, and the sooner it was begun the better.

The soldiers, weary from the march, were naturally more

ready to support Navarro than Ximenes, but the latter then addressed them with all his fiery eloquence, reminding them of the raids which had taken place along the Spanish coast and the many Spaniards who had been abducted and taken off to slavery – and who could say what torture and misery? He did not forget, however, to stress the wealth of their enemies and the booty which awaited capture. Then, because he himself was not interested in booty but in the souls of the Infidel, he went on to remind them – and perhaps the recording angel – that he came at the peril of his life in the service of the Faith.

The fleet bombarded the town, and the sea mist was of the utmost help to the Spaniards. Ximenes remained at Mazalquivir praying, while the soldiers went into action. In a few hours Oran had surrendered.

The conduct of the victorious soldiers was brutal. It is ironical to consider that they had marched forward under the sign of the cross. Murder, rape and pillage were hideously practised in the streets of Oran, and it was not until the men were weary of bloodshed, bloated with food and drunk with wine, stolen from the inns and houses, that they ceased inflicting these horrors on the unfortunate population of Oran. Then they lay snoring in the squares among the mutilated and the dead.

Four thousand Moors were said to have been slaughtered on that day, and between five and eight thousand made prisoners. Christian losses were said to have been slight.

Ximenes came in great joy to take official possession of the city, declaring that the victory was due to Christ. It was said that the day was fading as the battle began, but that a miracle took place and the sun stood still for several hours to allow the Christians to complete the slaughter. Four eye-witnesses bear testimony to the miracle. Prescott, commenting on it, says that it was an even greater miracle that the standing-still of the sun should have escaped the notice of Europe, where it must have been as evident as it was at Oran. The universal silence concerning this strange behaviour of the sun is certainly odd, but what seems equally remarkable is that these men could have looked on Oran and all the misery and suffering which had been inflicted on it, and tell themselves that their loving Father had made the sun stand still in order that it might be brought about.

Ximenes is said to have murmured: '*Non nobis, Domine, non nobis*,' as he blessed the army; but he was disturbed when he saw the corpses of men, women and children piled high in the streets. Navarro, we are told, reminded him that they were only Infidels. To which Ximenes replied, it was true that they were Infidels, but at the same time they were people who might have been made into Christians.

When one considers the means employed to make these people 'Christians', one wonders whether they were not after all fortunate to have fallen in the streets of Oran.

Ximenes now dreamed of setting the banner of the cross over every Moslem city, turning the inhabitants to Christianity, and introducing the Inquisition throughout all the dependencies of Spain.

However friction occurred between himself and Navarro, who told him that it was impossible for an army to prosper under a divided rule. He, Navarro, was the military man; Oran was captured, and Ximenes should return home; for fighting was for soldiers, not for monks.

Ximenes was not the man to avoid such conflict, and there is no doubt that he would not have gone back to Spain but for a certain letter which fell into his hands. Whether Navarro *allowed* this letter to be seen by the Cardinal is not known, but it is very possible. In it the King asked Navarro to do all in his power to keep Ximenes in Africa. 'Make use of him and his money', wrote Ferdinand. 'Keep him busy at Oran and, if there is no new enterprise to absorb his interest, invent something.'

This letter had the effect Navarro would have desired – supposing he had allowed it to fall into Ximenes' hands – and the Cardinal, fearful of what Ferdinand was doing in Spain, decided that he must return with all speed to what after all had first claim on his duty. He therefore declared that he was too old a man to endure the heat of the African summer, and on the 22nd of May he embarked for Spain.

Ferdinand made a great show of pleasure on receiving him, but Ximenes set no store by such pageantry, particularly as he had good reason to distrust the King's sincerity. So as soon as possible he made haste to Alcalá with his servants, certain gold and silver which had been taken from the mosques of Oran, and some Arab books for the university he was founding at Alcalá.

Ferdinand, delighted with the success of Oran, did not need the persuasion of Ximenes to continue with the African campaign. Consequently Navarro took Bugia in January 1510; and during the early months of that year, Algiers, Tennis, and Tremecen, together with several other towns, were captured by the Spaniards. In July Tripoli fell to Navarro; but in August he suffered a serious defeat in the Island of Gelves, and during this battle four thousand Spaniards were either killed or taken prisoner.

This put an end to the African campaign, and although Ximenes' dream of carrying Christianity to the Holy Land was not realized, the operations had brought several very important towns into the Spanish net.

As for the Count of Navarro, he was a professional soldier and, when his services were no longer required in Africa, he went to Italy and was engaged in the wars there. He was captured by the French; Ferdinand, who was too fond of money to part with it in ransoms for his subjects, left Navarro to suffer in captivity, a fact which so infuriated the count that he offered his services to France at the same time renouncing his allegiance to the King who had deserted him when he so desperately needed help.

Unfortunately for him, during a battle he was captured by the Spaniards and imprisoned at Castel Nuovo in Naples. He died there, by whose hand it is not certain. The gossipy Brantôme suggests that Charles V had him murdered; others believe he committed suicide.

Ximenes, back in Spain, ordered that agricultural labourers be brought home from Africa to deal with the harvest; he visited the families, in his diocese, whose members had been lost in battle or were still serving in Africa. He comforted them not only with words. The Cardinal's exchequer must have been considerably depleted, and it was no simple matter to get Ferdinand to repay him the money which had been lent for the campaign.

One of the clauses in the agreement which had been arranged between Ferdinand and Ximenes when the money had been advanced was that the loan should be repaid when the military operation was over, or that Oran should be joined to the See of Toledo which could then recover, over a certain number of years, from the great drain on its finances.

Ferdinand was against both methods of repayment. Those in whom the Cardinal had aroused a great deal of envy pointed out to the King that Ximenes had gained much from operations in Oran. Not only had he brought home rich booty but he had gained great glory; let that suffice.

Ximenes (as shown when he insisted on taking the benefice of Uzeda) was a man who could insist on his rights; and Ferdinand was unable to find a way out of his difficulties. Always at his worst when money was demanded of him, Ferdinand sent one of his servants to the Palace of Alcalá to make a valuation of all the booty Ximenes had brought home from Oran, that this might be set against the amount he had lent the King.

All that was found in the palace was a few carpets – the rest of the booty had not come into Ximenes' private possession; however, the value of these carpets was set against the sum Ferdinand owed.

Ferdinand was still anxious to see his son, the illegitimate Alfonso of Aragon made Archbishop of Toledo; and he chose this time to ask Ximenes if he would change Sees with Alfonso.

Ximenes was horrified, not only because he knew that Ferdinand's sole desire to appoint the young man was because he was his son, and this smacked of that flagrant nepotism which Ximenes had always declared he deplored, but because Alfonso was worldy in the extreme and quite unfitted for the post of Primate.

Moreover Ximenes himself (whether or not he had convinced himself, and with good reason, that he was one of the few men in the kingdom wise enough for the post) was determined not to give it up.

He declared that he would allow no such barter with the

84

dignities of the Church. If the King should suggest such an exchange to him again he would give up the Archbishopric and return to that cell from which Queen Isabella had taken him.

On returning to Spain Ximenes gave his attention to the Inquisition against which a charge had been brought to the effect that when comely women were taken into the Holy Houses on charges of heresy they were often violated by the Inquisitors.

Ximenes was naturally horrified at such scandal and decreed that any who were found guilty of these outrages should be sentenced to death. William Harris Rule, DD, states that none was put to death for this crime because none was convicted; and none could be convicted because none was prosecuted. 'Neither,' he continues, 'did the abomination cease.' Rule is of course fiercely anti-Catholic; and it is almost certain that had Ximenes found any of his Inquisitors guilty of rape (no matter who they were) he would have had them put to death.

We have an interesting sidelight on Ximenes's attitude towards women. He was sternly chaste; but that was not enough, for there were such evil rumours afloat concerning the clergy (often with good reason), and Ximenes was surrounded by men who would with the utmost willingness misconstrue any act of his which gave them an opportunity of doing so. Therefore, for the sake of the Church, Ximenes was determined to avoid any chance of scandal touching him.

When he went on his journeys he travelled without money and in the utmost humility, relying upon the hospitality of those who were prepared to give it. On one occasion, the Duchess of Maqueda, knowing he was passing her house, invited him to put up there for the night; she added that she herself would be absent but her servants would look after him. She knew full well that had she, a beautiful woman, not told him she would be absent he would have considered it unwise to accept the invitation.

However, the Duchess, who wished to talk with Ximenes on religion, had not left the house; she remained in hiding while her servants looked after Ximenes; and then, when he was preparing to retire for the night she came into the room.

Ximenes was angry; he rose, told the Duchess that she had deceived him, and that if she had anything to say to him the confessional was the place in which to say it.

Late as it was he walked out of the house.

One cannot help wondering whether such drastic behaviour was due to a certain temptation. If Ximenes had felt no interest whatever in the woman surely he could have taken a more gracious departure.

His attitude towards the *Beata* of Piedrahita is revealing, and an indication of the superstition of the day; it also throws an interesting light on the complexities of the human character. Here was a man, without doubt of great intellect, yet capable of childish reasoning (as shown in his campaign against the Mussulmans in Granada and Oran) and of amazing superstition, as shown in the case of the *Beata*. But perhaps the first instance is more surprising, for his conduct in Granada grew out of an injustice which was not to be expected from a man of high principles, while the blind faith of Ximenes which is such a part of his nature and was shared by many intellectuals had grown out of superstition.

In the year 1509 the devout woman (or *Beata*) of a small village in the diocese of Avila called attention to herself by her conduct. She was a peasant woman and someone had apparently trained her in mysticism, for she was capable of fasting for long periods of time. When she was a girl she had taken to the Dominican habit, and she became known for her sanctity. Mysticism was beginning to be practised in Spain and, according to Francisco de Villalobos, who wrote in 1498 and was physician to Ferdinand, many mystics came from Italy and were called *Aluminados*; they claimed to have special powers which enabled them to see into the future, and that visions appeared to them in which coming events were revealed. Villalobos declared that the *Aluminados* should be driven from all houses and kept without food, that they should be put into prison or scourged from the towns.

However there were many people who were impressed by the prophecies of these people, and Ximenes was apparently one of them, for in 1493, when he went to Gibraltar in his capacity of

86

Provincial of the Franciscans, he wished to cross to Africa as a Christian missionary, which would have meant certain death. A *Beata* spoke with him, told him that she had had a vision of his greatness and the good he could bring to both the state and the Church; she advised him against rashly throwing away his life; and Ximenes had listened to her and followed her advice.

Now came the *Beata* of Piedrahita with her extraordinary stories. She declared that she was the Bride of Christ and that there was physical contact between them. She went into trances, and lay on the ground arms outstretched, so that her body had the form of a cross. There were times when she assured her listeners that she *was* Christ. She talked with Christ and the Virgin as though they were with her – she speaking for all of them; and often her listeners heard conversations such as this when the *Beata* was passing through a church doorway: 'The bride of my dear Son should go before me.' That was supposed to be the Virgin Mary speaking. The *Beata* would reply: 'But if you had not borne Christ I could not have been His bride; the mother of my husband should have the greater honour.'

It was all very impressive and the *Beata* through long practice was able to go without food and to endure great privations.

There were many people who were shocked by the woman's revelations of the intimacies she enjoyed with Christ, and these demanded that she be brought before the Inquisition, as surely blasphemy such as hers was the worst sort of heresy.

The case was so important that it was brought before the Inquisitor-General himself. Ximenes having questioned the woman declared that she was truly wise and saintly. However, there were still many who were not satisfied, and demanded that the matter be brought to the notice of the Holy See.

Julius II, who had succeeded Pius III in 1503, sent Giovanni Ruffo of Friuli and the Bishops of Burgos and Vich to examine the *Beata*, with a command that if they should find the woman to be guilty of fraud she should be punished with the utmost severity, but in such a manner as to subdue the scandal.

The *Beata* was discharged, and it was assumed that a decision had been made in her favour. Llorente however states that she was later taken before the Inquisition but escaped through the favour of Ferdinand and Ximenes.

The case of the *Beata* of Piedrahita gave rise to a new assumption; this was that those who gave themselves up to prayer and fasting could be filled with divine spirit which would manifest itself in trances and a gift of prophecy. Naturally enough there were others who wished to attain notoriety in the manner in which the *Beata* had.

There is one recorded instance (Lea in his *Religious History of Spain*, who quotes Vicente de la Fuente's *Historia Eclesiástica de Espagña*) of a Franciscan friar of Ocaña. The custodian of the Franciscan province of Castile reported this case to the Inquisitor-General. It appeared that the friar declared that after much prayer and fasting he had been rewarded by a vision, in which God had appeared and told him that he had been selected to beget a race of prophets on numerous holy women. These prophets would reform the world.

This was too much even for the superstitious to accept, and the unfortunate friar was taken to a dungeon and there given such 'active treatment' that it was not long before he was made to see that the visions (if any) he had experienced had come not from God but from the devil.

At the Cortes of Aragon in the year 1510, complaints were made against the Inquisition when it was stated that the Inquisitors were seeking to take over civic administration of justice. They intruded into all courts on the pretext that religious laws had been broken; they were adding to the number of their officials and, as these were exempt from taxation, the country was being deprived of more and more revenue. Any man who tried to point out the error of their ways – whatever his rank – was penalized even to the extent of excommunication. Ferdinand, who was presiding over the Cortes on this occasion, was asked to limit the power of Inquisitors and restore the laws and rights of the people of Aragon.

Ferdinand promised to look into these matters; but the Inquisition was powerful and there were two years of procrastination before certain amendments were made.

State affairs occupied the mind of the Inquisitor-General to a great degree. The league of Cambrai had been signed by Louis XII, Ferdinand, the Emperor Maximilian and the Pope; Venice had been attacked and defeated. Ferdinand had quarrelled with his one-time ally, Louis, and sought to make Pope Julius and Henry VIII of England his allies against the French King. Henry VIII had already married Catalina, widow of his brother, Prince Arthur, and was prepared to follow the advice of his father-in-law Ferdinand, which he received through his wife, for at that time Henry did not regard Catalina with the disgust he was to feel in later years.

Louis, realizing that Ferdinand was preparing to strike against him, attacked first; he invaded Papal territory, took Bologna in May of 1511 and planned to elect a new Pope in place of Julius whom he accused of bringing war to Europe, breaking promises and simony (that accusation which could often be applied with truth to Popes).

Julius called on Ferdinand for help; and Ferdinand withdrew his forces from Africa preparing for a campaign in Italy against the French. As for Ximenes, he was eager to protect Julius who had made him a Cardinal, and was ready to hand over a large sum of money towards the defence of the Pope.

Fighting began at the end of 1511, and the French under Gaston de Foix, Duc de Nemours (whose sister was Ferdinand's wife, Germaine) won some quick victories in the north of Italy. Ferdinand and his allies were disconcerted; but quite suddenly Gaston de Foix was killed in battle and the French, so disturbed by this fact, withdrew from Italy in June 1512.

Ferdinand had made Naples secure for Spain, and then turned his attention to Navarre. The Queen of Navarre at this time was Catherine who was a granddaughter of Ferdinand's half-sister Leonora, and Ferdinand had once tried to annex Navarre by peaceful methods when he had endeavoured to arrange a match between his son, the Infante Juan, and Catherine. This had failed, largely through the machinations of Catherine's mother who, being French, insisted that her daughter should marry Jean d'Albret, a Frenchman.

Spain's hostility to France gave Ferdinand the opportunity

he needed and before the year was out he was master of Navarre; and in these great plans Ximenes was close beside his master, but he did not relax his grip on the Inquisition.

In 1515 the Cortes of Toledo, as had that of Aragon, asked that the Inquisitors should be prohibited from interfering in secular courts, and this was granted by the King, for neither Ferdinand nor Ximenes wished for an outbreak of rioting. Ximenes contented himself with setting up the Inquisition in Oran and making plans to send out his Inquisitors to the New World.

The New Christians, who were being persecuted so cruelly, believed that if the names of those who bore witness against them were published, they would have a greater chance to prove their evidence false. But the wicked law of the Inquisition which demanded secrecy in the tribunal, was one of its strongest weapons and it was clear that if it were abandoned it would not be so easy to 'prove' persons guilty of heresy.

The New Christians, knowing this and knowing also that the King's love of money was one of his strongest characteristics, offered Ferdinand 600,000 ducats if he would rescind that law and order that the names of witnesses should be published.

Ferdinand, as ever finding the impulse to take money irresistible, was on the point of agreeing; there was however, the Inquisitor-General close at hand. He put down a large sum of money which, if it was not as great as that offered by the New Christians, was enough to turn the King from granting their request.

Ximenes was certain that the Inquisition was necessary to Spain and, if he desired to put a stop to the evil practices of certain of its officers, he was determined not to relax any of the harshness meted out to its victims.

In fact Ximenes shows clearly (as at Granada where he had no compunction in breaking his country's solemn treaty) that where the extirpation of heretics was concerned he was without conscience or humane feelings. He must have realized that the appalling injustice imposed on victims by the secrecy of the tribunal was barbarically cruel; but what did he care for that? To his fanatical mind all that mattered was that heretics should die; and if, by some evil chance, those who were not heretics suffered in the process, he would reason as others had reasoned before him: If they died the fiery death they had nothing to fear. God would know them for members of the Catholic Church when they arrived in heaven, and for that reason their place there would be ready for them.

Ximenes did not fear death or discomfort; therefore he had no sympathy to spare for others who suffered that fear.

In the year 1515 Ferdinand's health began to fail; he was suffering from a very bad heart and dropsy. There were times when he was unable to walk and had to be carried from place to place in a litter. He was sixty-three but he still hunted when he felt well enough to do so. In December he was staying with the Duke of Alva near Placencia, and on leaving him he travelled through Andalusia until he became so ill that he was forced to rest at the village of Madrigalejo near Truxillo.

Ferdinand was very suspicious of the presence of Adrian of Utrecht, who was chief adviser to his grandson Charles and who, he rightly suspected, was there because he, Ferdinand, was not expected to live, and at such a time it was necessary to have one who was devoted to Charles' interest close at hand.

There was some anxiety in the kingdom, for Charles, the heir, was a boy of only sixteen who had been brought up in Flanders in the care of his aunt Margaret, the sister of his father Philip the Handsome, who was also the widow of his uncle the Infante Juan.

Charles' brother Ferdinand was three years his junior, and Ferdinand was the favourite of the King. This was natural enough, for the boy who was his namesake had been brought up as a Spaniard, whereas Charles was looked upon as a foreigner in Spain.

In spite of Ferdinand's determination not to accept the approach of death it was necessary that his affairs should be in order, and although he refused to have Adrian of Utrecht admitted to his presence because, as he said, the man had come to see him die, there came a time when his doctors could no longer keep the truth from him.

Ferdinand had made a will in 1512, and in this he had appointed young Ferdinand Regent of Castile and Aragon during his brother Charles' absence. He also left to his namesake the grand mastership of the military Orders of Alcántara, Santiago and Calatrava.

That was more than three years ago, yet young Ferdinand was still only thirteen years old, and the counsellors felt it incumbent upon themselves to point out to the dying Sovereign that such an arrangement was impossible. A boy of thirteen could not possibly be accepted as Regent of Spain. There was, Ferdinand was advised, only one man who should be given the post: Ximenes.

Ferdinand was silent and turned his face away from those present. It must still have rankled that Isabella had chosen this man of humble origins and raised him up above Ferdinand's own son, to be the 'third King of Spain' as Mendoza had never been. Yet Ferdinand knew that he was dying; he knew that his beloved grandson could never shoulder all the responsibilities which would fall to him; he was also fully aware of the stern qualities of Ximenes and the needs of the country which he loved.

He therefore slowly nodded his head and said that they were right, for Ximenes was an honest man, who had no family to push forward into high places; Ximenes would be a grateful man, always remembering that he owed his good fortune to Queen Isabella, and would therefore act to the best of his power in the interests of her young grandsons.

His advisers then assured him that he was wrong to separate the grandmasterships of the military orders from the crown, for Isabella had incorporated these with the crown to the great advantage of the country.

Ferdinand wept, and muttered that his grandson would be poor indeed; to which his advisers answered that Ferdinand would be the brother of the King, and what better good fortune could he possess than that?

The succession was therefore fixed upon Juana and her heirs, and Ximenes was to be Regent of Castile until Charles came to Spain. Ferdinand did manage to leave the governing of Aragon, until the return of Charles, to his illegitimate son, the Archbishop of Saragossa, which must have delighted him for he had certainly schemed earnestly, and had boldly faced the disapproval of Isabella to win favours for that young man.

He died in the early morning of the 23rd January, 1516, and his body was laid beside that of Isabella in the Alhambra. On the completion of the Metropolitan Church they were both taken there, where Charles eventually caused a white marble mausoleum to be built.

For the second time Ximenes was Regent of Castile. From the beginning of the Regency he came up against opposition, for Adrian of Utrecht declared that Charles intended to appoint *him* Regent. Ximenes was not the man to give way lightly, and eventually an arrangement was made that he and Adrian should share the Regency until Charles' further instructions should arrive. Charles was no doubt advised about the superior capabilities of Ximenes for very soon instructions did arrive from him to the effect that the Cardinal was to have full authority; but at the same time the young Prince made it very clear that he had the utmost confidence in Adrian; and since Adrian was a man who wished to keep the peace, Ximenes allowed him to remain within his counsels so that it appeared that the Regency continued in their joint hands.

Charles then announced his desire to be crowned King. This was difficult, for Juana, though living almost a prisoner in Tordesillas, was still Queen.

The suggestion was strongly opposed, not only by Ximenes but by the royal council. Sixteen-year-old Charles however was determined to have his way.

If he took his advice, Ximenes wrote, he would not, out of respect for his mother, persist in his conduct.

But Charles was ready to take no one's advice on this point; he wanted to be called King and he was determined he would be; and realizing that nothing else would satisfy him Ximenes ordered banners to be set up containing the words: *Real, real real, por el Rey Don Carlos nuestro Señor*.

The people of Spain were somewhat unenthusiastic because they considered that the son was being disloyal to his unfortunate mother.

However, Charles had his way, as he was to have it so often in the future.

Ximenes at this time was eighty years old and his vigour and courage were astonishing. There was almost certain to be trouble at such a time and in such circumstances, and undoubtedly there would have been but for the strong hand of the Cardinal.

Ferdinand, beloved of his grandfather, a favourite of Ximenes, had expected to be placed at least equal with his brother in his grandfather's will; and there were many at his little court to cluster about him and seek to make a revolution. His elder brother, who could not even speak Spanish and who was under the influence of his paternal grandfather, the Emperor Maximilian, would not understand the customs of Spain; it was only to be expected that there were many who would have preferred to see the younger brother – every inch a Spaniard – on the throne; and one day when Ferdinand was hunting and met a hermit in the forest who pretended to be a wise man and assured him that he would one day be King of Castile, the boy was ready to take his stand at the head of a revolt.

But Ximenes was a hand. However fond he was of the boy who had been brought up at Alcalá, he did not forget his duty. He may never have seen Charles, but Charles was the true heir to the throne, and Ximenes was going to keep that throne for him until he returned to Spain.

Therefore he decided to set the Court in the centre of Spain where he could be within easy reach of any district in which trouble might arise. He chose Madrid – in his own diocese of Toledo – and from that day the town assumed a new importance in Spain.

Ximenes' attention was continually focused on young Ferdinand and he never allowed the boy to make long journeys from Madrid. He was determined that Castile and Aragon should remain united, and if, as some hoped, Aragon were given to Ferdinand and Castile to Charles, Spain would have taken a step backwards in her history to those days before the country had been united by the two great Sovereigns. Therefore Ximenes was determined to save Spain for the young man whom he had never seen and to curb the ambitions of that other youth for whom he must have had some real affection.

So this man, at that great age, ruled Castile as Regent for Charles who on his part was Regent for his mad mother; and in addition to these onerous state duties he did not forget that he was Grand-Inquisitor of Castile.

During his term of office the harshness of the Inquisitors had not abated in the least; Ximenes was as determined as any of his predecessors to wipe out heresy.

The New Christians, now that Spain had a new King who was not imbued with Spanish ideas and had been brought up among the Flemish, let their hopes rise. Surely such a King would not show the same favour for the Inquisition as his grandfather had. They therefore renewed an offer which they had once made to Ferdinand – and how near Ferdinand had been to accepting it – to pay a large sum of money to Charles if he would introduce fresh legislation into the Inquisition. They asked once more that the rule of secrecy might be abolished and that those who were accused might have an opportunity of facing those who had given evidence against them, as was the custom in civic courts.

Charles was ready to accede to this request, but Ximenes was as fierce in its denunciation with Charles as he had been with Ferdinand.

If a person were to be confronted with the one he accused of heresy, demanded Ximenes, who would be willing to be an informer?

The practice must never be introduced. Ximenes foresaw a dearth of victims if it were.

Ximenes won the day. Charles was ready to accept the advice of his counsellors; he was only sixteen but already aware of his great responsibilities and his ignorance of the country which he was called upon to rule.

Prescott points out that Charles 'showed a facility to be directed by those around him in early years, which gave little augury of the greatness to which he afterwards rose'. But surely this willingness to be directed is a certain augury of the greatness to come, for Charles even at sixteen was wise enough to be aware of his own ignorance.

It was twenty months after Ferdinand's death when Charles came to Spain. Ximenes by this time was failing in health. Pope Leo X hearing of his condition, wrote to him reminding him that he was past eighty years of age and that he should allow himself more comfort. He should not sleep in the coarse garment of the Franciscans and should have a bed to replace his pallet. Leo ordered him to take more comfort, for his services to the Church could be replaced by no other.

Ximenes was quite indignant when he read this letter, crying out that he had worn the Franciscan habit for the greater part of his life, and was now ordered to give it up. It is certain that he disobeyed this command of Leo's.

When he knew that Charles had landed in Spain his spirits rose so much that it appeared to those about him that he had regained his great energy and would live for many years.

On the 26th of September he went to the monastery of La Aguilera not far from Aranda, and in early October he was well enough to say Mass and take supper with the monks. Charles had made no great haste to meet his Regent, and news was brought to Ximenes that he intended to visit Aragon before coming to Castile.

Charles' Flemish followers who hoped to rule him were anxious that he should not meet Ximenes, for they were certain that the powerful personality of the old man would have a deep and abiding effect on their young King; and Charles, according to some chroniclers, was prevailed upon to write to Ximenes that famous letter, amazing in its ingratitude, which has been said to have broken the heart of Ximenes and hastened his death.

It is not absolutely certain that the letter was written, although there is mention of it by all contemporary sources.

In it Charles was reputed to have thanked Ximenes for his services as Regent and named a place where they could meet that Ximenes should give him counsel; when he had done this Ximenes was to leave Court for his diocese and there live in retirement, seeking from Heaven the rewards which Heaven alone could give.

This was all the new King had to say to the man who had served his grandfather and grandmother faithfully and to whom the present peaceful state of the country was due.

It is difficult to imagine the heart of Ximenes being broken, as some writers suggest. At the same time this must have been a bitter blow to him, for Charles could not have stated more clearly that he had no further need for his services.

Ximenes died in his house at Roa to which he had gone in order to be near the new King. His death took place, only a few days after he received the letter dismissing him, on 8th November, 1517, when he was eighty-one years old.

His last words, we are told were: *In te, Domine, speravi.*

Ximenes was one of those men whose mingling love of austerity and harshness made the Spanish Inquisition what it was. Without his piety he could not have commanded respect; without his harshness he would have reformed the cruel laws of the institution. But although he believed in justice and was eager to rectify the guilty conduct of his inquisitors he was as eager as any who had gone before him to maintain the harshness of treatment towards heretics. There is no doubt, of course, of his good intentions. He was certain that he wanted nothing for himself. As a statesman he worked for the State and as a churchman for the Church. Would he have been a greater man if he had suffered from the human foibles of, say a man like Mendoza? He would certainly have been a more lovable one.

One can respect Ximenes (taking into consideration his times and, in understanding that cruel bigotry, forgive it) but one cannot feel any affection for him.

He was clearly a brilliant man; there is no doubt that the work he did for his country was admirable. He really did intend to suppress nepotism, that persistent failing of his day (and of our own) when an important office was given to a man not because he was fitted for it, but because of the influence he had been able to command. Yet he had a softness for his own family. Bernardín got off very lightly after attempting to murder him; and Juana de Cisneros the daughter of Juan, his brother, was the object of his interest and attention. Juana, being the niece of the rich and powerful Ximenes was a good *partie* and there were many noblemen of Castile who were eager to marry her. Gonzalo Mendoza, the nephew of the Duke of Infantado, was one, and on this match Ximenes smiled, until he discovered that the Duke's motive in arranging the marriage was to take Gonzalo's estates from him and give them to his own son, for, he reasoned, the husband of the niece of rich Cardinal Ximenes would be wealthy enough.

Ximenes then, instead of smiling, frowned on the match. Gonzalo and his niece were too young for marriage, he said; and this was true, for the prospective bride and bridegroom were eleven and thirteen respectively; however their very youthful state had not troubled the Cardinal until he had discovered the intentions of Infantado to rob the boy of his estates.

Later a more satisfactory match was arranged for Juana with Alfonso, son of the Count of Corunna.

So, in spite of Ximenes' horror of nepotism he was not averse to arranging affairs to the advantage of his family.

He never sought to hide the fact of his humble origins; indeed, he so frequently alluded to them that once again he might be considered to lay himself open to the accusation of pride – pride in his great rise to power from such humble beginnings. So mixed were his motives that it is not easy to know the man.

There is a story that on one occasion a preacher attacked those churchmen who flaunted their extravagance before the world in fine garments. Ximenes was at this time wearing an ermine robe and the discourse was directed against him. He could not however resist taking the preacher aside and showing him, beneath the rich ermine, the patched and threadbare Franciscan robe.

Why should Ximenes have bothered to show this man the coarse habit? What did it matter what such a man thought of him? But the pride of Ximenes was great and his humility was so bound up in pride that it is often difficult to separate the two.

The story goes on that beneath *his* coarse monk's habit the sancitmonious preacher was wearing fine linen.

On the death of Ximenes a box was found among his possessions which contained the needles and thread with which he was accustomed to darn his habit; but why there should have been great virtue in this it is difficult to see. Surely a man such as Ximenes could have been better employed in the service of his fellow men than with needle and thread.

As a matter of fact his time was often occupied with other matters, matters which brought upon his head the reproof of the generations to come; I refer to his activities with the Inquisition.

In 1516, he, eager to carry the work of proselytizing in lands beyond Spain, appointed Juan de Quevedo Bishop of Cuba and made him the first Inquisitor in those lands.

A case against Juan de Covarrubias, who had died, was brought to his notice during those last months of his life. The penalty was the digging up of Juan de Covarrubias' bones, decking them out in the *sanbenito* and giving them to the flames. But this man had been a friend of Pope Leo's, who sought to defend him from the infamy of public burning and save his estates for his family.

Ximenes, however, was determined to punish heresy which had been proved by his Inquisitors; and there was conflict between Leo and Ximenes when the latter received that important letter from young Charles; Ximenes died with the case of Juan de Covarrubias still unsettled.

He is praised by many who declare him worthy of sainthood. But reflect for a moment on an account of the numbers of his victims: 3,564 burnt at the stake; 1,232 burnt in effigy; and penitents who suffered from confiscation of worldly goods and other punishments, 48,059.

These figures may not be exactly accurate; but let us suppose they were somewhere near the truth.

Fifty-two-thousand people is a large number; one can be sure that every one of these would be very doubtful of the claim of Ximenes' admirers that the latter was a saint.

What can we really know of this man? Not a great deal. We can though be sure of this: under his guidance the Inquisition firmly planted by Torquemada became that sturdy growth which was so firmly rooted in Spanish soil that it was able to exist through the seventeenth and eighteenth centuries and into the nineteenth.

CHAPTER SIX

MARRANOS AND MORISCOS

From 1507 there were separate Inquisitions of Castile and Aragon; and when Ximenes was appointed Inquisitor-General of Castile, Juan Enguera, Bishop of Vich, became Inquisitor-General of Aragon. In 1513 he was followed by Luis Mercader, Bishop of Tortosa, on whose death in 1516 Fray Juan Pedro de Poul, Dominican Provincial of Aragon, took over his post. Fray Juan however died in the same year and was succeeded by Adrian of Utrecht, Cardinal and Bishop of Tortosa.

After the death of Ximenes the Inquisitions of Castile and Aragon were united and Adrian of Utrecht became Inquisitor-General of both Castile and Aragon, and continued to hold this post until 1522 when he was elected to the Papacy.

Up to this time the victims of the Inquisition had been mostly the Marranos and the Moriscos, but eight days before the death of Ximenes Martin Luther had nailed his theses to a church door in Wittenburg and in addition to Jews and Moors, who had been baptized and were suspected of returning to the faith of their fathers victims were to be discovered among those who embraced Lutheranism.

Although there had been a general exodus of Jews in 1492, this unfortunate race still provided the majority of victims for *autos de fé*. Many of these came into the country from Portugal where, on their expulsion from Spain, they had settled in 1492. However when Isabella, daughter of Isabella and Ferdinand, married Emanuel, King of Portugal, she had declared she would not set foot in Portugal until Emanuel had sworn to follow the example set by her parents and expel from his territory all those Jews who would not embrace Christianity. Emanuel had foreseen the stupidity of following this policy but he had given way, for a match between Spain and Portugal could have succeeded in uniting the peninsula under one crown, and that crown could fall to the heirs of himself and Isabella.

Emanuel, however, not wishing to lose a valuable section of his subjects, sought to convert the Jews to Christianity; he used bribery and force. His confessor, Jorje Vogado, urged him to take very stern measures, and he ordered that all Jews who refused baptism must leave the country, except children of under fourteen who were taken from their parents to be forcibly baptized. Emanuel hoped that many parents, realizing that they would lose their children if they left the country, would accept baptism as the only alternative, and thus remain.

This decree caused great anguish to many families and some even killed their children rather than let them fall into the hands of the Christians.

When those Jews who had remained loyal to their own religion were preparing to leave the country, Emanuel sent preachers among them in a last effort to convert them; and when this failed, he imprisoned them until the time limit for departure had been reached. Then he offered them slavery or baptism. They were driven to the churches and, if they refused baptism, attempts were made to force it upon them with threats of torture, or torture itself. Thus in Portugal there were living many Jews who were called Christians; they had been given Portuguese names, but many of them had in secret reverted to their old Jewish names and gave them to their children.

In Portugal, as in Spain, the Jewish community began to prosper financially and thus aroused the envy of the people among whom they lived. There were outcries against them and pogroms occurred; yet still they prospered and multiplied.

It was a source of great irritation to the people of Portugal that King Emanuel, having forced Christianity upon the Jews who remained in Portugal, had given them some concessions. In 1497 he had promised them that they should be immune from the Inquisition for twenty years. He had also promised that all accusations of Judaism should be brought within twenty days of the alleged acts having been committed and that the trial should take place in accordance with the secular law. This meant that any charged would be brought face to face with their accusers—a concession which New Christians in Spain had long and in vain sought to establish, even offering large sums to their sovereigns in exchange for it. In Portugal the property of a condemned man was not confiscated as in Spain but was allowed to be enjoyed—by his heirs.

The promise that they should not be treated as a separate race in the kingdom, given at the same time, was broken two years after it was made, when a law was introduced forbidding them to leave Portugal without permission, or to sell their lands.

In 1506 there occurred the terrible massacre of Lisbon. This began when one of the New Christians entered a Dominican church at Eastertide. He happened to glance at a crucifix, which was reputed to have magical powers, and lightly express his doubts of its holiness.

The mob, always envious of the prosperity of the race, was ready to wreak its malice. The unfortunate New Christian was seized by the hair and dragged from the church into the street. In a very short time he was torn to pieces by the 'Christian' mob.

That however did not satisfy them. They formed into a procession, and the Dominicans (eager to set up the Inquisition in Portugal) urged them to take vengeance on these New Christians who had accepted baptism and who, they were sure, practised Judaism in secret, The mob needed little urging. They thronged the streets, entering the houses of the New Christians, robbing, murdering and committing every atrocity they could conceive. The massacre continued for three days and nights. and would not have ended then had it not been impossible to find more victims. Thus several thousands were killed because of a careless remark of one man. But the mob was still ready to be roused, ever watchful, determined, since the King had promised the New Christians leniency and there was no Inquisition established in their kingdom, to take the law into its own hands.

After the massacre certain hardships were abolished and New Christians were allowed to trade, and leave or come into the country as they desired.

In 1512 the exemption from persecution was extended to 1534, but in 1515 Emanuel did consider setting up the Inquisition in Portugal. He tackled this matter half-heartedly however, and when certain difficulties arose he allowed it to drop.

This was great good fortune for the New Christians who continued to prosper and, as they had in Spain, marry into noble families and even take up posts in the Church itself. Spanish Jews seeking refuge from the rigours of the Inquisition naturally found their way to Portugal.

This state of affairs lasted during the reign of Emanuel, but when John III, who followed him, married Catalina, the sister of Charles V, in 1525, greater pressure was brought to bear on this twenty-year-old King to set up the Inquisition in Portugal.

Clement VII agreed to absolve the King from his promise not to set up the Inquisition until the term agreed to had expired, and sent Fray Diogo de Silva as Inquisitor to Lisbon.

The arrival of Diogo in Lisbon gave rise to an outcry among the New Christians who sent an emissary to Rome – Duarte de Paz, a New Christian of great wealth and persuasive powers. Meanwhile Clement died, and Paul III who succeeded him at first hesitated but later agreed to set up the Inquisition in Portugal. Thus in 1536 it was established there; the New Christians in spite of their wealth and power had managed only to delay it for a few years.

The first Lisbon *auto de fé* took place on 20th September, 1540; others were to follow. Thus it was that many New Christians of Portugal thought to better their lot by slipping across the border into Spain and settling down in obscurity.

Later to be a Portuguese Jew living in Spain was to rouse immediate suspicion; thus even after the great exodus there were many *Marranos* to supply victims for the Inquisition.

It was hardly to be expected that the Moors who had been forced to accept baptism should have been any more free from the suspicion of reverting to their old religion than were the Jews.

The zealous officers of the Inquisition needed victims, and

the *Moriscos* provided as productive a source as did the *Marranos*.

In 1526 certain descendants of the old Kings of Granada, approached Charles and asked his help against the officials of Granada who ill-treated them and their kind in direct opposition to the treaty which had been signed at the time of the surrender of Granada.

This step was the worst the *Moriscos* could have taken, for the commission, which Charles had set up to look into these matters and which was led by the Bishop of Guadiz, reported to Charles that the attention of the Inquisition should immediately be turned on Granada.

In spite of past promises the Inquisition was installed in that town. The familiar pattern began to take shape, beginning with the term of grace for all those who would come forward voluntarily to confess their heresy.

People were now urged to commence spying on one another. It was not necessary for *Moriscos* to perform actions which obviously proclaimed them to be Mohammedans, such as observing the fast of Ramadan, or circumcising their children, praying with faces turned to the East or indulging in baths; they could be condemned for abstaining from the eating of pork and the drinking of wine, or for staining their nails with henna, or singing Moorish songs, dancing Moorish dances, refusing to eat animals which had died a natural death, or even because of the way they slaughtered animals for food.

These customs were listed for the use of Inquisitors and those who must spy for them.

New laws were made for the *Moriscos*. They must leave their doors open when they were celebrating weddings or on feast days, so that at any moment a spy could mingle with them to discover if they were following any custom which would make it necessary for them to be brought before the Inquisitors. There must be no wearing of Moorish garments; Arabic must not be taught or used; at every birth a Christian midwife must be in attendance.

These new laws sent shudders of alarm through the *Morisco* population; they had the terrible example of the Jews before them. They called together their leading citizens and it was agreed to offer Charles 80,000 ducats if he would withdraw the edict.

There was now no Torquemada nor Ximenes to lash the King to scorn, and Charles accepted the money, and suspended the edict 'during his pleasure'. There was however a tax called *farda* which must be paid for the wearing of Moorish garments or the use of Arabic. This brought in a sum of 20,000 ducats to the treasury.

But the Inquisition was established in Granada and the first *auto de fé* was held in that city in May 1529.

On this occasion a proclamation was made in which it was explained that the Lord Inquisitors Apostolic of the city had determined to celebrate an Act of Faith in honour and reverence of Jesus Christ for the exaltation of the Holy Catholic Faith and Evangelical Law and the extirpation of heresies.

A recorder of the times (an official of the Inquisition whom Rule quotes in Vol. 1 of the *History of the Inquisition* from *Auto General de la Fé Exaltacion de Su estándarte catolico, etc.*) reports that the pious population of Granada heard this publication with breathless attention, and welcomed it with Catholic demonstrations of ardent religion, their eyes being 'covered' with 'liquid sparkles of tenderness' as they came out very reverently to listen.

By the time the great day arrived the population must have been in a suitable state of excitement. Rule gives a list of the chief actors in the drama (Vol. I. *History of the Inquisition*). They are as follows:

1 Heretical *alumbrado*. (Blasphemous hypocrite)
1 Forger of passports in the Name of the Inquisition
3 Bigamists
3 Witches
33 Jews who had been baptized but who had been discovered practising Judaism
22 Jewesses accused of the same
2 Mohammedans
7 Effigies of Judaizers who had escaped (Men)

10 Effigies of Judaizers who had escaped (Women)
 1 Effigy of a Mohammedan who had done likewise

These were all penitents who would be required to become reconciled to the Church and suffer some penalty — severe enough, but not death at the stake.

Six Jews however were in the party under this sentence, and the people of Granada were to have their first smell of burning human flesh.

The six condemned to the flames were three men and three women. Five of them lost heart at the sight of the faggots and were garrotted before the flames consumed their bodies; but one man held out to the end and as a consequence suffered the terrible penalty.

This was Rafael Gomez. The chronicler records of this brave man: 'Thus died that infinitely miserable Hebrew and, giving his being to the ashes, delivered his unhappy name to the mute horror of time, and his sacrilegious memory to the eternal night of oblivion.'

In this first *auto de fé* it is interesting to note that only two Mohammedans figured, and one effigy, presumably for minor offences since they were not among those condemned to death.

The *Moriscos* of Granada, full of alarm, pointed out this fact to the authorities of the Inquisition, declaring that the Inquisition could find so little against *Moriscos* that it should therefore be withdrawn from those quarters in which the population consisted almost entirely of converted Moors.

This was an unfortunate suggestion, for the officials of the Inquisition were determined not to be withdrawn or suspended. They had worked hard to set their feet on the soil of Granada, and there they intended to remain. It had never been difficult for them to find charge against *Marranos* — why should it be against *Moriscos*?

The *Moriscos* responded, as the *Marranos* had done, with further offers of money to the King as bribes in order that they might live in peace. Charles, a practical man, was always ready to accept these offers, and because of this the *Moriscos* were able to buy their peace.

During the reign of Charles they were able to ward off disaster by these bribes; and it was only when Charles' son, Philip II, came to the throne that they found at the head of the State one who was immune from bribery and an even more fanatical supporter of the Inquisition than his great-grandmother, Isabella, had been.

It was after the accession of Philip, therefore, that the *Moriscos* provided so many victims for the Inquisition.

CHAPTER SEVEN

MARTIN LUTHER

At that time when the Catholic Church through the Inquisition was fighting so desperately to retain supremacy in all lands, there arose in Europe its greatest menace.

For several years before Martin Luther pinned his famous theses to the door of the Wittenburg church there had been certain rumblings throughout the Christian world which showed the dissatisfaction of many people with the existing ecclesiastical doctrines.

So often when people consider the Inquisition at work they imagine Protestants being tortured and burned at the stake by Catholics; but it is a fact that the number of Protestants who became victims of the Inquisition was small compared with that of the Jews and the Moors.

For as long as the Inquisition existed the Jews suffered from it; but Protestantism in Spain itself was of shorter duration; and was almost eliminated in forty years.

The Reformation could be said to have begun in the early part of the sixteenth century, about one hundred years after the Council of Constance which put an end to the Great Schism of the West and elected Martin V Pope – and incidentally passed the death sentence on Huss and Jerome of Prague. By the sixteenth century learning had spread through the printed word and was no longer confined to members of the clergy; and when such as Reuchlin, Melanchthon and Erasmus sent forth their works into the world, food for thought was given to a great number of people. Erasmus, the most famous of these, while perhaps not himself a great reformer, certainly did more than any other to prepare the minds of men for the acceptance of the Reformation.

His satires on the vices practised in the Church were far

more effective than fulminating would have been; and thus it was that he prepared the way for Martin Luther.

Pope Leo X wished to raise money; and he chose the by no means original method of doing so by the sale of Indulgences. He might announce that he wished to use the money so gained for holy purposes such as war against the Infidel or the re-building of St Peter's in Rome, but when he received the money he could use it for whatever purposes he needed it most.

Popes who had practised these somewhat dishonest methods in earlier days had not had to contend with the more enlightened population of the early sixteenth century.

Sir Thomas More (in *Utopia*) and Erasmus (in *Christian Prince*) had both condemned unfair taxation. In *Praise of Folly* Erasmus had even gone so far as to refer to the criminal habit of bestowing false pardons. Yet it was typical of the rather timid nature of Erasmus, who was no fiery reformer such as Martin Luther but a man who preferred to remain in the background, lightly pointing out anomalies and prodding others to act, that he should add that he did not include Indulgences in his criticism unless they were false, it being no affair of his to dispute the rights of the Pope. He did, however, go on to say that people who relied on pardons were encouraged to commit crimes.

However, the writings of these men were enough to set the people wondering whether pardons granted simply because the Pope was in need of money, even for a holy war or the building of a cathedral, had any value.

The amount realized from Indulgences did not all find its way to Rome, for a 'commission' was granted to the sovereigns in whose lands the pardons were sold. There can be no doubt that this was a painful necessity as far as Rome was concerned, but it is certain that without such a system it would not have been easy to raise the money.

When John Tetzel, the Dominican friar, who had won fame by the clever way in which he was able to dispose of Indulgences, was appointed by Leo X to raise the money for St Peter's by further sales, Charles V was able to raise a loan of

175,000 ducats on what he hoped to draw from the sales in his territory.

Tetzel passed through Germany in great pomp. When he and his associates came to a city, he would send on his deputy to announce his coming. The deputy would present himself at the house of the magistrate with the words: 'The Grace of God and of the Holy Father is at your gates.'

Immediately the church bells would peal and the whole town would turn out to greet them, from the highest dignitaries of the churches to the smallest of the children; all carried tapers, and the processions would be escorted to the church.

At the head of this procession was the Pope's 'Bull of Grace', which was carried on a cushion made of velvet and cloth of gold. Immediately behind the cushion came the bearer of the great red cross followed by men swinging censers.

When they reached the church it was Tetzel's duty to mount the pulpit; and almost like a barker at a fair he would begin to extol the virtues of Indulgences.

They were the most precious of all God's gifts. The cross which his supporters carried was a symbol of the cross on which Christ had been crucified, and as a blessed symbol had all the holiness of that other cross. If they paid him they should have pardons, not only for the sins they had committed, but for the sins they intended to commit.

He compared himself with St Peter. He would not change places, he declared, for he, by the sale of Indulgences, had saved more souls even than St Peter had by his preaching.

There were Indulgences for all sins. Even the most violent sin conceivable could be pardoned, providing the sinner was ready to pay in accordance with the enormity of the sin.

Indulgences could also be bought for the dead. Let them reflect. Was there some loved one who at this moment was writhing in hell fire? And they had the power to save that loved one from further torment by purchasing for him an Indulgence! 'For twelve groats you can deliver your father from purgatory. What fate do you think will await *you* when you die if you neglect to make this sacrifice?'

Did they not understand that God had ceased to reign and

had given all his powers to the Holy Father? Thus could the Pope give them eternal salvation – if they bought their Indulgences.

Tetzel was a business man. He had his tariff. Royalty and heads of the Church paid twenty-five ducats for an ordinary Indulgence. Counts and barons paid ten. Others paid according to the reduced scale of their incomes. But the price naturally rose in proportion to the size of the sin. Polygamists received absolution for six ducats; murderers paid eight ducats; those guilty of witchcraft, two; and so on.

Tetzel arrived at Juterbock four miles from Wittenburg; and in Wittenburg was the man who was ready to sweep away the old Church and found a new one.

In the year 1483, in the little town of Eisleben in Saxony, Martin Luther was born. His family was poor but his father, John Luther, believed in the advantages of learning and wished his son Martin to have a better chance than he himself had had. Therefore when Martin was fourteen he was sent to the Franciscan school at Magdeburg. Here Martin suffered great hardships. The teachers were cruel, and he was timid; moreover he was one of the poorest of the scholars and was often forced to beg his bread. Martin tells a story of how one Christmas he and some other poor scholars went out to sing carols in the hope of earning a little food. A farmer hearing their singing called to them, but his voice sounded harsh to the boys, and so accustomed were they to ill-treatment by their masters that they ran away, and only when the farmer ran after them, calling them to come into the farm where they would be fed, did they stop and enjoy his hospitality.

It was this timid boy who was to shake the Western hemisphere with his doctrines and who was capable of the great courage necessary to such a reformer.

When he passed from Magdeburg to a school at Eisenach he once again went carol-singing and it was thus that he was seen by Ursula, the kindly wife of Conrad Cotta, who noticed his hungry looks and how poorly he was clad – and perhaps she saw some light in his face which she recognized as potential greatness, for not only did she give him food on that occasion but she insisted that he lodge in her house, free of charge.

This was a great opportunity for Martin, who now need not concern himself with feeding and clothing his body and could give himself entirely to his studies. He loved music and learned to play the lute and the flute; he composed music, and it is significant that this music should take the form of martial hymns such as *Ein feste Burg ist unser Gott* and *Komm Heil'ger Geist, Herre Gott.*

When he was eighteen Luther was sent to the university of Erfurt to study law, and here it was soon recognized that he was exceptionally clever. It is said of him that he spent all his spare time in the library of the university and one day whilst there he discovered the Bible. He had never before seen a Bible and was surprised to find how much it contained of which he had never heard. He had always believed that what he had heard read in churches comprised the entire Bible.

He went back and back again to the library and always to the Bible.

Luther obtained degrees of Master of Arts and Doctor in Philosophy, but he did not, as had been intended, take up law; instead when he was nearly twenty-two years of age he entered a religious order: the convent of St Augustine in Erfurt.

The family was furious; it must have been a great blow after the sacrifices both they and their son had made to acquire an education; they could not see into the future.

In his convent he practised those privations which were considered necessary to produce sanctity, and learned to go for days without food or drink. One day, having carried abstinence from food and drink too far, he was discovered in his cell in a state of unconsciousness.

He was eventually appointed teacher of physics and dialectics at the university of Wittenburg, where he learned Greek and Hebrew in order to enable himself to make a closer study of the Bible. He lectured on the Bible, and crowds came to hear him; and later the title of Doctor of Divinity was bestowed upon him.

It was when Tetzel was in the neighbourhood of Wittenburg

that Luther's indignation became so great that he could no longer remain silent.

He expressed his indignation when people came to him and told him that they could sin as much as they liked because they had just purchased an Indulgence and their salvation was therefore assured. He declared that there could be no forgiveness of sins without full repentance and the determination not to sin again.

Tetzel, furious at the interference, denounced Luther.

Then on the 31st October, 1517, one day before the festival of the Elector's new church of All Saints, when many pilgrims were gathered there in the hope of acquiring Indulgences, Luther walked up to the church door and nailed on the posts his list of ninety-five Theses which were an outcry against the sale of Indulgences.

Those who had come to buy their salvation were astonished to read:

'When our Lord and Master Jesus Christ says "repent", he means that the whole life of believers on Earth should be a constant repentance.'

'The Pope is unable and desires not to remit any other penalty than that which he had imposed of his own good pleasure, or conformably to the canons, i.e. the papal ordinances.'

'They preach mere human follies who maintain that, as soon as the money rattles in the strong box, the soul flies out of purgatory.'

'Those who fancy themselves sure of salvation by Indulgences will go to perdition along with those who teach them so.'

'We should teach Christians that he who gives to the poor, or lends to the needy, does better than he who buys an Indulgence.'

'The Indulgence of the Pope cannot take away the smallest deadly sin, as far as regards the guilt of the offence.'

'The bishops pastors and theologians who permit such things to be told to the people, will have to render an account of them.'

'This shameless preaching, this impudent commendations of Indulgences, make it difficult for the learned to defend the dignity and honour of the Pope against the calumnies of the preachers, and the subtle and crafty questions of the common people.'

In a very short time first Germany then Europe was talking about these Theses of Martin Luther. Leo X was not inclined to take them seriously. Tetzel however was furious at this attempt to stop the money rattling into the strong box. He announced that Martin Luther should be burned at the stake; and he had a scaffold erected on which he publicly burned Luther's Theses in place of his body.

In 1518 Luther appeared at Augsburg to answer charges brought against him, and conducted himself with such courage and skill that it was impossible for the Papal authorities to bring a case against him.

By 1520 a Papal Bull forbade any country to accept the teachings of Luther.

The Reformation had begun, and those followers of Martin Luther were to provide a fresh supply of victims for the Inquisition.

CHAPTER EIGHT

THE PROTESTANTS OF VALLADOLID AND SEVILLE

There are some countries which could not be nationally Protestant, and others which could not be nationally Catholic. The Germans and the English are natural Protestants (it is due to the character of the people) while the French, Italians and Spaniards are natural Catholics. The emotional, almost sensuous, ritual of the Catholic Church is more suited to the Latin than the Nordic races. For this reason there was never any great danger of Lutheranism gaining a hold in Spain.

However in April 1521, Adrian of Utrecht, the Inquisitor-General, sent out a command that all Lutheran books in Spain be seized.

There must have been some demand for these books for in 1524 a ship, which came from Holland and was bound for Valencia, was captured and brought into San Sebastian. Lutheran books were discovered among the cargo and publicly burned. Venetian ships also brought books into Granada; these were seized and burned and the captain and crews of the ships imprisoned.

In 1528 a Ghent painter – Cornelius – was brought before a tribunal for denying the heresy of Luther and existence of purgatory, and declaring that no good purpose was served by confession.

Cornelius was no martyr, and was quickly made to assure the council that he had been drunk when he had made such fantastic statements and that, although when he was in Flanders he may have listened to such foolish talk, now that he was in Spain he fully realized its error. He was not burned at the stake, but merely sentenced to perpetual imprisonment.

Hugo de Celso, a doctor of Burgundy, was another Lutheran

who tried to introduce his beliefs into Spain. He was tried at Toledo and was later burned at the stake.

Another would-be reformer, Melchor de Württemburg, came to Valencia to do what he believed was his duty. He went through the streets, on a preaching mission, urging all whom he saw to repent, for the world was on the point of destruction. He told his hearers that he had travelled to Germany to confer with the Lutherans and consider whether their doctrines held the answer of which mankind was in need. The mention of Lutheranism made authority prick up its ears, and Melchor was brought before a tribunal. His wild stories of the end of the world were not, it was decided, the result of deadly sin; it was only if he was tainted with the dreaded Lutheranism that he would be considered worthy of the flames. Melchor quickly denied all belief in Lutheranism and consequently escaped with a whipping.

An early Protestant martyr in Spain was Francisco de San Roman of Burgos. In his youth he visited the Netherlands on business, and while there he became an adherent of Lutheranism. He was clearly a very earnest man for he quickly felt it to be his duty to convert Charles V himself and, nothing daunted by the enormity of this task, made an attempt to accomplish it. He bearded Charles at Ratisbon and for his pains was made a prisoner and sent to Spain that the Inquisition might deal with him.

There, since he refused to revert to the Catholic Church he was condemned to the flames; and in the *quemadero* suffered the additional torment of having his body pierced with swords by those spectators who had congregated for the pleasure of seeing a man burned alive.

There were two danger spots to the Catholic Church in Spain from Protestantism in the middle sixteenth century: one of these was in Seville and the other in Valladolid.

The community in Seville had been founded by Doctor Juan Gil known as Dr Egidio who was a canon-magistral of Seville Cathedral. During his lifetime he was accused of Lutheran tendencies and as a result was sentenced to a term of imprisonment in the Castle of Triana. When he was released he travelled to

Valladolid and there exchanged views with others of the Reformed Faith. Fortunately for Dr Egidio he died before there was any great outcry against Protestants.

When Dr Egidio died his place in the magistral canonry was taken by Doctor Constantino Ponce de la Fuente, a man who had acted as confessor and chaplain to Charles.

The Prior of the Geronimite house of San Isidro, Maestro García Arias, known as Doctor Blanco, was an important man who had also become interested in Lutheran ideas. He was in a position of influence, for the brethren under his command rather naturally began to share their Superior's interest in the reformed religion and thus the numbers of converts began to swell.

Francisco de Zafra, another influential churchman who was able to bring in many converts, also joined the group, which now began to have among its members people from every walk of life. There was Don Juan Ponce de Leon who was related to the Dukes of Arcos; at the other end of the scale were two brothers who were rag-pickers, Francisco and Antonio Cardenas.

Such activities could not be allowed to go on undisturbed and it was not long before the Inquisition received secret information concerning the Geronimites of San Isidro. The fact that an investigation was pending was somehow conveyed to certain of the monks, who, knowing full well the methods of the Inquisitors, were not going to fall into their hands if they could help it.

Therefore some of them slipped away. Two who did so were Cassiodoro de Reina and Cipriano de Valera. That they escaped was fortunate because both these men achieved fame by their writings: Cassiodoro became head of the Protestant Church, Spanish and French, in Frankfurt, Antwerp and London. He translated the Bible into the Castilian tongue (which has been reprinted and circulated in modern times). Cipriano de Valera wrote *Los dos Tratados del Papa y de la Misa* which was published in London in the year 1588 and again in 1599, and was reprinted once more in 1851 and contained in his work *Reformistas antiguos Españoles*. He also translated the *Institutio* of Calbin. (Lea.)

But the flight of these men only served to increase suspicions, and the writings of Doctor Constantino Ponce de la Fuente were seized by the Inquisition. As a result some of his books which had been in circulation for many years were condemned to be confiscated.

A pastor of Geneva named Juan Pérez de Pineda had in the meantime been preparing books on Lutheranism which he wished to send into Spain, and there was one very brave convert who undertook to see that they were delivered. This was Julianillo Hernández. He was a Spanish deacon of a Lutheran church in Germany and he was evidently seeking martyrdom in undertaking such a task. He was a little man and as a result he became known as Julianillo *el chico*. He equipped himself as a muleteer and made his journeys between France and Spain, carrying goods among which were hidden the books he wished to smuggle into Spain.

In July 1557 he arrived in Seville and, not daring to go into the city, waited outside its walls for Don Juan Ponce de Leon to come to him and collect them.

A fatal mistake occurred during one of these expeditions. The books were delivered to those who it was known could be trusted, but it appeared that a staunch Catholic priest possessed the same name as one of the reformers and he received the books intended for his namesake. The Catholic priest lost no time in getting into touch with the Inquisition.

The mistake was discovered almost as soon as it had been made and Julianillo and Don Juan lost no time in leaving Seville.

But the mischief was done. Arrests were numerous; moreover both Don Juan and Julianillo were captured before they could leave Spain.

Then began the slow and painful task of collecting information, which was conducted with that formality so beloved of the Inquisition, and the prisons were soon full to overflowing.

Eventually even Doctor Constantino and Dr Blanco were languishing in the prisons of the Inquisition.

While all this was happening in Seville the Inquisition had had news of that other little colony in Valladolid. The head of this group was Don Carlos de Seso, reputed son of the Bishop of Piacenza who had become a Reformist. He quickly made converts; among these was the Bachiller Antonio de Herrezuelo and his wife Leonor de Cisneros. Another was Juan Sánchez who became so wildly zealous that he was a danger to his friends. He had been a favourite preacher of Charles' who had taken him with him to Germany and it may have been during one of these visits that he had become a member of the Reformed Faith.

When Sánchez came to Valladolid he entered the household of Doña Catalina de Hortego and converted her. Pedro de Cazalla, the parish priest, had become an ardent Reformist, and he, with his sisters Doña Beatriz and Doña Costanza de Vivero, and his brothers Agustin de Cazalla and Francisco and Juan de Vivero, conducted meetings in the house of their mother Leonor de Vivero.

It was impossible for this state of affairs to exist for many months without discovery. The people had been taught by the Inquisition that the only way in which they could escape suspicion was to spy for the Church. One of the converts was Doña Ana Enríquez, a daughter of the Marchioness of Alcañizes; and a certain Christóbal de Padilla, who was her steward, evidently talked too much. He was arrested and the group, realizing they could place little reliance on his discretion, were deeply alarmed.

Escape was almost impossible for already the Inquisition was alert; some however attempted it. The only one to achieve it was Sánchez, but a year later he was caught and brought back to trial.

The Inquisitor-General at this time was Valdés, Archbishop of Seville. Valdés looked upon this discovery of Protestants in Valladolid and Seville as an excellent opportunity. He badly needed not only the distraction this would offer to the people, but to show the King how important was his own position in the land. He was on the verge of disgrace and this affair seemed as though it might have the effect of setting him back in favour.

The King, Philip II, was at war and urgently needed money; he called on his subjects for this and, as the King was in Flanders, the Princess Juana, Philip's sister, who was then Governor of the Kingdom, demanded 100,000 ducats as Valdés' contribution.

Valdés was not prepared to pay, and this brought a reproof from Charles V now in retirement at Yuste. Valdés however, while knowing that by refusing the royal request he was placing himself in jeopardy, could not bear to part with his money, first declaring that he had none, then that money obtained from priests for the purpose of war would prove unlucky, and that all Philip needed was God's help, not that of his priests.

Philip meanwhile sent instructions that Valdés was to be banished from Court although he might be given an opportunity to retire of his own accord.

Thus, with the discovery of Protestants in Seville and Valladolid, Valdés no doubt felt that he had a chance to show how useful he could be to the State and keep both his money and his position. He therefore set about working up a scare. He arranged that stories of hair-raising orgies, which were reputed to have taken place in the houses of the reformers, should be circulated throughout the country.

Meanwhile Juana, the mad Queen, died and Princess Juana, as Governor of the Kingdom, commanded Valdés to convey her body to Granada. This Valdés refused to do. The burial could wait, he said; he had work of the utmost importance to perform in Seville and Valladolid.

The discovery of the Protestants completely changed the attitude of Charles and Philip towards Valdés, as the Inquisitor-General had known it would. Instead of being asked to leave the Court he was now commanded to stay.

Charles in Yuste, close to death, was deeply disturbed. He wrote to Juana — and a copy of the letter was sent to Philip in Flanders — assuring her that there should be no leniency shown to Protestants, who could grow into a great menace to the country.

The results of the investigations were the notorious *autos de fé* of Valladolid and Seville.

The first of these took place on Trinity Sunday, 21st May,

1559; and in this suffered the first of the Valladolid prisoners.

Valdés, determined to make a great show of his own import-ance through the Inquisition, had the *auto* proclaimed fifteen days before it was to take place; and he put armed guards on the prisons because, he let it be known, so great was the Luth-eran menace that he feared an uprising to free the prisoners.

The day before that fixed for the *auto* there took place the ceremony which consisted of carrying a bush to the *quemadero*. Officials left the Palace of the Inquisition and when they reached the square of the town a banner was unfurled; on this was inscribed an order forbidding any person to carry arms from that moment until the *auto* was at end, and ordering that no one should ride through the streets either on horseback or in a carriage while the procession passed.

After the procession of the bush came that of the Green Cross. Then the friars of the neighbourhood, who had as-sembled at the prison of the Inquisition, emerged with the *al-guazils* and other officials, all carrying white tapers. In the centre of the procession was a bier covered by a pall. The men chanted as they walked to the square where the ceremonies of the next day would take place. There the scaffold would already have been erected, and on this scaffold was the altar. Then the pall would be lifted from the bier to disclose the Green Cross draped in black veiling. It was erected on the altar, and the Dominicans in the party then kept watch during the night while the rest of those who had made up the pro-cession went home.

The next day was that of the great occasion. The victims were assembled, their heads and beards closely shaved, some in coarse black coats and trousers without shoes or stockings, most in the *sanbenito*.

The *auto* of Trinity Sunday 1559 was one of special note, not only because in it some of the Valladolid Protestants suffered, but because it was the first in Spain to be attended by Royalty. Princess Juana, sister of Philip II, who was governing the country during her brother's absence, was present and with her was the Prince, Philip's son, Don Carlos.

The presence of these two made it a very glittering occasion, for with the Royal party came many of the courtiers, and galleries of great magnificence were set up.

The procession of victims was headed by the dead body of Leonor de Vivero. Fortunately for this woman she had died during the trials, but under torture several people had said that she had entertained Lutheran opinions and had allowed her house to be used for meetings of Lutherans. Therefore her body was dug up, arrayed in the *sanbenito*, the *caroza* set upon her head, and she was carried through the streets to the *quemadero* where she was publicly burned.

The house which had been used for the meeting place was burned to the ground and a pillar set up inscribed with words to the effect that during the pontificate of Paul IV and the reign of Philip II, the Holy Office of the Inquisition condemned the house of Pedro de Cazalla and his wife, Leonor de Vivero, to be razed to the ground since in it the Lutherans had assembled to hold meetings against the Holy Catholic Faith and the Church of Rome, 21st May, 1559.

Another victim was Leonor's son, Doctor Agustin de Cazalla, who was Canon of Salamanca. He had denied a leaning towards Lutheranism but under the rigours of the torture chamber he had broken down and confessed begging for the opportunity to be reconciled to the Catholic Church. The Inquisitors, having no intention of sparing his life, allowed him to hope that this might be done, assuring him that for his soul's sake he must confess more and give more information concerning other people who had been involved in the community of Protestants. When he said that he could give no more information he was brutally told that he was to die on the next day. He therefore prepared himself to die, saying that he must do so without falsehood on his lips, and only by uttering falsehoods of the worst kind could he implicate others.

His brother, Francisco de Vivero, was also a priest, being a curate of Hormigos. Like his brother he denied that he was Lutheran until submitted to the torture, when he broke down and confessed, imploring reconciliation with the Church.

During the reading of the sermon in the great square the two brothers were placed side by side on two of the highest seats reserved for those who were considered to be guilty of the greatest heresy; and there they sat while the sermon, of one hour's duration, was delivered by Melchor Cano. The oath to protect and aid the Inquisition was roared out by the spectators, and the crowd then took up the cry 'To the death!' The two priests were put upon asses and thus conveyed to the Plaza de la Puerta del Campo, the *quemadero* of the occasion, and there they were burned, both preferring to deny Lutheranism for the sake of strangulation before death.

Their sister, Doña Beatriz de Vivero, who had been tortured, was also strangled and burned.

Alfonso Perez, a Master in Theology, Christóbal de Ocampo, a Knight of the Order of St John and Almoner of the Grand Prior of Castile and Leon, and Christóbal de Padilla were all strangled first and then given to the flames.

Another who suffered was Juan Garcia, a silversmith. It was his wife who had discovered where he was meeting his fellow Lutherans and had betrayed him to the Inquisition. He was strangled and thrown to the flames; she was awarded a pension – as a good child of Holy Church.

Juana Blasquez, a servant of the Marchioness of Alcañizes, Catalina Roman and Isabel de Estrada, the last a *beata*, were all strangled first and burned afterwards. Perez de Herrera, a magistrate, and Gonzalo Baez, a Portuguese, were other victims dying in the same way.

The true martyr on this occasion was the Licentiate Antonio Herrezuelo, and the story of him and his young wife is a particularly pathetic one.

This advocate from Toro was a braver man than any of his friends. When he had accepted the Lutheran doctrines he had accepted them for life, and no fear of physical torture could shake him. He had recently married a young and beautiful girl, Leonor de Cisneros, and together they had studied the new ideas and discussed them earnestly. They both came to the conclusion that Lutheranism was the true religion.

Leonor however, twenty-three years old, with plans for a happy future in her mind, was seized by the *alguazils*, separated from her husband and dragged to the 'Holy House' for questioning. She was submitted to all the gruesome stages of torture devised by the founders of the Inquisition and when she – so young, so full of life – was shown those hideous instruments which could ruin a young woman's beauty in a very short time, could maim her for life and submit her to the most hideous pain conceivable, she gave way and agreed that she had listened to Lutheran ideas and implored to be reconciled to the Church.

For this she was saved from the *brasero* and preserved for perpetual imprisonment in the *casa de la penitencia*.

Meanwhile her young husband was determined to remain true to his faith. He refused to implore forgiveness; he accepted Lutheranism as the true religion, he declared, and he was ready to die for his belief. He was therefore condemned to the flames without the blessing of strangulation before burning.

On the way to the *quemadero*, his friends urged him to save himself from the hideous death of being burned alive; it was of no avail. He sang hymns as he was paraded through the streets and quoted passages from the Bible. Nothing annoyed the mob more than a show of such courage in the face of the most hideous of deaths. Naturally it shook their belief in their own righteousness. How could a man go almost joyfully to die for his beliefs if those beliefs came from the devil? Therefore, because they were shaken and filled with certain self-doubts, they wished to vilify the martyr. Antonio Herrezuelo's journey to the *quemadero* was a very painful one for him.

Since he insisted on singing hymns and quoting the Scriptures the painful gag was put into his mouth. Even so, he presented such a calm face to the crowd that he only succeeded in infuriating them. As the faggots were about to be lighted, one of the soldiers, so maddened by the calm of the martyr, thrust his halberd into the victim's stomach; but this brutal act was not enough to kill him and put him out of his misery, it merely increased his pain.

All this Antonio Herrezuelo bore with fanatical calm, showing that to die for his faith was a glorious experience.

Meanwhile Leonor remained in the house of the penitents, for ten years in a state of terrible remorse. With the passing of each day life became more intolerable and eventually Leonor knew that she could not endure to live in her present state. There seemed to be only one course open to her; she must follow her husband. She therefore confessed that she was a relapsed heretic, knowing that there was only one punishment for such: death by burning. She was tried again and condemned to the flames.

Even now, if she implored reconciliation at the last moment, she might be strangled before the faggots were ignited. But this time Lenor was determined to die as her husband had died. There was no recantation. She was burned alive on 28th September, 1568, nearly ten years after the death of her husband.

On this first of the famous *autos de fé* of 1559, fourteen people had been condemned to the flames. Sixteen others had been found guilty of minor offences – some to be sent to the galleys to endure a number of years, perhaps a lifetime, of humiliating toil and frequent applications of the lash; some to be stripped to the waist and paraded through the streets, whipped as they went; others to stand in the squares that the self-righteous mob might heap upon them any indignity they cared to.

This *auto de fé* is remembered, not only because in it suffered some of the first of the Protestant martyrs, but because Princess Juana and Don Carlos, Prince of the Asturias, had been present and had been required to swear allegiance to the Inquisition.

There is no doubt that Don Carlos did this with an ill grace. It may have been that he felt it to be a great indignity for the heir to the throne to swear an oath of fidelity to any, even the Inquisition; and poor crippled Don Carlos was deeply conscious of his dignity. It may have been that at this *auto de fé* his sympathy with the Protestants, which was to bring a great deal of inconvenience in the future to himself and others, was born.

The second *auto de fé* was held at Seville on 24th September, 1559. This was another of those grand occasions and three days before it people began to gather in the town. The setting was as magnificent as it had been at Valladolid and the Duchess of Bejar brought a party of friends to view the spectacle. She had a very special interest because her kinsman, Juan Ponce de Leon, was to be burned, and she longed to see this done.

Don Juan Ponce de Leon was the most distinguished of the victims on that day. He had been an ardent Protestant and he had never thought that he would be taken to the *quemadero*, always believing that his family connections and his wealth would save him from such a fate. It must have been a bitter disappointment to find that his influence availed him nothing, apart from bringing the Duchess to the show.

Although there was no royalty present on this occasion the great crowds which had been assembling and the presence of the Duchess, and of course the fact that Lutherans were to be burned, made it an outstanding *auto*.

Don Juan Ponce de Leon, the aristocrat, had, when he realized that the Inquisition was on the track of his Lutheran community, been one of those to escape; he had made some progress but as he had been on the point of embarking for England the officers of the Inquisition had caught up with him. Chains were put about his arms and legs, an iron cap was placed over his head and shoulders, and attached to this cap was a loop which went into his mouth and held his tongue down. In this painful condition he was brought back to Seville.

He was a brave man however and was determined to remain true to the religion he had adopted. Torture could not make him swerve and he was abandoned to the secular arm. When he was brought to the *quemadero* the gag still remained in his mouth distorting it horribly, and a recorded description says that the appearance he presented was so grotesque that he seemed scarcely human. No doubt the noble Duchess enjoyed the spectacle.

On this occasion twenty-one people were condemned to the flames, and eighteen to do penance. There was one effigy which was condemned to the flames. This was that of Francisco de Zafra. Francisco, a presbyter of the parish church of St Vincent of Seville, was a man of great learning and skilfully he had managed to hide his interest in Lutheranism. But he was foolish enough to entertain in his house a *beata* who soon discovered a great deal about his ideas and the people whom he was meeting in order to discuss them. This *beata* became hysterical, and Francisco de Zafra put her under restraint, an action which so enraged the woman that as soon as she was free she went to the Inquisition and told them of Zafra's interest in Lutheranism. She gave the Inquisitors lists of names; and when Zafra was questioned, he insisted that the woman was mad; but meanwhile with their accustomed zeal, the Inquisitors had made many arrests, had shown their prisoners the persuasive machines in their secret chambers, and very soon they were on the way to uncovering the greatest Protestant heresy as yet heard of in Spain.

Zafra was arrested; fortunately for him so numerous were the prisoners that there were not enough prisons to contain them and insecure ones had to be used. Into one of the latter Zafra was put, and in a very short time he had escaped. It was for this reason that his effigy, not his person, was taken to the *quemadero* on that tragic September day in Seville.

Several people died bravely on that day. There were Don Gonzaler, a great preacher, and his two sisters. He had been tortured with the utmost severity, but nothing could make him deny his faith. He was condemned with his sisters to be burned alive and, when the fires were lighted, instead of asking the mercy of strangulation in exchange for recantation, these three brave people sang together: 'Hold not thy peace, O God of my praise; for the mouth of the wicked and the mouth of the deceitful are opened against me; they have spoken against me with a lying tongue.'

Rule says these three people died in the faith of Christ and of His Holy Gospel; by which he means that they died in the Protestant Faith. Whether they accepted one dogma and refused another seems unimportant compared with the overwhelming and admirable courage with which they were able to face the fire, sacrificing their lives for the right to their own opinions.

Fray Christóbal de Arellano and his two brothers also went as martyrs to the flames. Fray Garcia de Arias, an elder monk of the monastery of San Isidro of Seville, was another martyr.

Christobal de Losada, who had practised as a physician in Seville, and Fernando de San Juan who was a schoolmaster, also were burned alive.

Morcillo, a monk of the monastery of San Isidro, was less brave. At the last moment he wavered and received strangulation before his flesh was consumed.

Another victim was Doña Maria de Bohorqués, who was nearly twenty-one years of age. She was the illegitimate daughter of a nobleman of Seville and had been well educated.

She was arrested, and calmly admitted her interest in the new ideas, but would not mention the names of others. She was taken to the torture chambers and there put to the torture, and in a weak moment she admitted that her sister Juana, although aware of her interest in Lutheran doctrines, had not protested nor tried to turn her away from them. When she was taken to the *quemadero* and the iron was placed about her neck at the stake, she was ordered to recite the creed. She obeyed, but her manner of doing so betrayed her adherence to Lutheranism, and afraid of so much courage, her tormentors strangled her. One feels relieved that she received this small mercy.

The Inquisitors lost no time in arresting Maria's sister Juana for, they insisted, had she been a good Catholic not only would she have reproved her sister for her heretical leanings but she would have reported her to the Inquisition. Juana was pregnant at this time and, with a show of great magnanimity, the Inquisitors did not torture her. They waited until her child was born, and eight days later took it from her; after another week she was taken down to the torture chambers. These wicked men were able to devise especial torture for a woman recently recovered from childbirth, and in addition to their usual cruel practices they passed cords about her breasts gradually tightening them until they cut into the flesh hoping that in her anguish she could be induced to betray her husband and her friends. Her ribs were crushed in the process and her poor mangled body was taken back to its dungeon. Mercifully she died within a week.

The most famous of all the *autos* of this year was the one which took place on 8th October. This is notorious because Philip II himself took part in it.

A contemporary recorder, a Flemish official, states that there were two hundred thousand spectators. This was another of the Protestant *autos*, for there were among the victims only one relaxed Morisco, one Judaizer reconciled to the Church and two other penitents convicted of minor offences, while there were no less than twenty-six Protestants.

Philip had made a vow when he had come near to shipwreck. His fleet had begun to founder within sight of Laredo, and then he had solemnly declared that if God would save him and his ships he would, as a reward for the Deity, take the utmost vengeance on the heretics in Spain. Philip came safely out of the adventure and lost no time in keeping his vow.

With the King came his son, Don Carlos, Prince of the Asturias, and his sister Juana – in the cases of the two last this was their second *auto* of recent date. Philip's presence naturally brought out many other great personages, and the *auto* was attended by the Prince of Parma, the Archbishop of Seville and among other high prelates the Bishops of Palencia and Zamora. Ambassadors from France and Rome represented those places and thus gave their implicit approval of the fierce attack on the new religion.

The sermon was preached by the Bishop of Cuenca; and this occasion was made even more remarkable because during it Philip took the oath of allegiance to the Inquisition. This he did in all humility with bared head and ungloved hand, drawing his sword and brandishing it as he swore.

The most distinguished of the victims on this day was Don Carlos de Seso who was forty-three years of age and had spent many years in the service of the Emperor Charles. He was recognized as one of the leading Lutherans and was certainly a very brave man, for on the day before he was to die – and it does not need a great deal of imagination to picture the state of mind of people, who had been weakened by torture, suddenly to learn that the last terrible ordeal was immediately before them – he asked for pen and paper and when it was given him wrote a full confession of his faith; he affirmed that the doctrine of the

Catholic Church was not the true faith and that the one in which he was fully prepared to die was the living faith.

Such men were disconcerting. They must have presented a noble sight on their way to the *quemadero*, an alarming inspiration to those watchers in the crowd. For this reason men like de Seso were burdened with the additional torment of the gag.

De Seso had been so acutely tortured that he was unable to stand whilst listening to his sentence, and it was necessary for two *alguazils* to stand on either side of him and hold him up. One story is that this brave man, when the gag was removed from his mouth, found himself not far from the Royal gallery. He lifted his burning fanatical eyes to the cold blue ones of Philip and asked him how he could allow such horrors to take place within his kingdom; to this the King, burning with righteous indignation against heretics, having within the hour, in the face of the world, declared his determination to support the Inquisition with heart, mind and soul, replied: 'I would myself bring the wood to burn my own son if he were guilty of heresy as you are.'

It is not difficult to picture that dramatic scene: Philip, cold as he ever was, so certain that he had God on his side; the maimed martyr; and the glowering cripple who was already aware of his father's dissatisfaction with him and already learning to hate him.

De Seso is reputed to have shown no fear of the flames and to have told the crowd that if he had had time he would have convinced them that they should follow his example. But as this would not be allowed, he continued, he begged his tormentors to light up the fire as quickly as they could, for he was ready and eager for it.

And this was the case, for when the faggots had been lighted and the rope which bound him to the stake had burned through, eagerly he threw himself into the heart of the fire.

There was only one other martyr on that occasion; this was Juan Sánchez who had escaped to Flanders. Like de Seso he called for more and more fire and seemed to revel in his agonies.

The other victims took advantage of the rule to be reconciled to the Church of Rome, and for this they received the mercy of strangulation before death. One woman did manage to commit suicide by cutting her throat with a pair of scissors. The Inquisition took revenge on her by burning her effigy.

There took place another *auto de fé* in Seville on 22nd December, 1560, and at this suffered many of the Protestants who had been gathered into the Inquisition's net when the enquiries had started in Seville and Valladolid.

On this occasion thirteen people were burned with three effigies, and thirty-four were condemned to penances.

The effigies were those of Dr Juan Gil (Egidio) and Dr Constantino Ponce de la Fuente. The first had died a natural death but Doctor Constantino had not been so fortunate. He was arrested and put into a dungeon which was so small that it was impossible for him to move, and there he was kept until he died of dysentery. He is reputed to have exclaimed: 'Oh my God, were there no Scythians, no cannibals, nor beings even more cruel than these in whose power You could have left me rather than to have made me the prisoner of these barbarians?'

The bodies of these two were brought from the grave to be burned with their effigies on 22nd December, 1560.

One of the victims on this occasion was that Julianillo Hernández, who had been living peaceably in Frankfurt and had brought the books to Spain in the hope of introducing Lutheranism to that country. He was an exceptionally brave man and during his three years in prison had been submitted to the vilest tortures, yet never had he betrayed any of his friends. He had shown the utmost defiance towards his jailors and is reputed to have chanted, after they had left him in his cell:

> '*Vencidos van los Frailes, vencidos van;*
> *Corridos van los lobos, corridos van.*'
> '*There go the friars, there they run!*
> *There go the wolves, the wolves are gone.*'

This bold chanting voice, heard in the corridors of the grim prison, struck chords of new hope in many fainting hearts. It was men like the little Julianillo Hernández who were the greatest danger to the Inquisition.

Naturally he was brought gagged to the *auto* but, when at the last moments the gag was removed and he was besought to implore reconciliation with the Catholic Church and thus escape burning alive, he reproved them for such suggestions; and stretching out for a burning faggot he held it near his head that he might be consumed the quicker.

This *auto de fé* is made more interesting by the fact that among the victims were a Frenchman and two Englishmen.

A little is known of the case of one of these Englishmen who appears in the records as Nicolas Bertoun (presumably Nicholas Burton).

Burton was a Londoner who sailed the seas and had often called at Spanish ports in the course of business. About two years before this *auto* took place he had landed at Cadiz and there he had talked too freely of his beliefs, for he was arrested by an *alguazil* and brought before the Inquisition. Naturally when he was arrested his ship and all her cargo were confiscated; it is probable that this rich booty was one of the main reasons for Burton's arrest.

He was not told on what grounds he was imprisoned, but he was kept in a dungeon for two years.

Meanwhile the owners of his ship were eager to recover their property, and they despatched another Englishman, John Frampton, to Spain in order to discover what had happened to Burton. Every obstacle was put in Frampton's way and eventually he himself was arrested on the charge of having a heretical book in his luggage.

Frampton was tortured and, not being able to withstand this form of persuasion – as Burton was – he agreed to become a Catholic. Frampton was sentenced to more than a year's imprisonment, and all his possessions were confiscated; he was to wear the *sanbenito* for a year and was never to leave Spain. Meanwhile Burton was condemned to the flames and was burned alive.

Nothing is known of William Brook, except that he was a

133

sailor from Southampton, nor of the Frenchman Barthélemi Fabienne, except that they were also burned at the stake.

In the next *auto* which took place on 26th April, 1562, there were forty-nine victims who were Lutherans. and twenty-one of these were foreigners. In October at another *auto* there were thirty-nine Lutherans. These numbers were not great when compared with those of the Marranos and the Moriscos, the reason being that Lutheranism did not take a firm hold on Spain, and the risings in Valladolid and Seville were the only ones of any note.

But the *auto de fé* was becoming a common spectacle throughout the country, no more unusual than a bull-fight and having very much the same appeal to public taste.

CHAPTER NINE

ARCHBISHOP CARRANZA

One of the most important victims of the Inquisition during the Protestant persecution was Bartolomé de Carranza y Miranda, Archbishop of Toledo and Primate of Spain.

His case is an indication of the insecurity of every man in Spain during that era.

It seems incredible that a man of such high position, of such influence and importance, could be dragged so low; but such was the power of the Inquisition.

Carranza was born in the year 1503 at Miranda de Arga in the kingdom of Navarre. His parents were of noble status and when he was fifteen he was sent first to the university of Alcalá, and later to the college of St Balbinia, to study philosophy.

When he was eighteen years old he took his vows in the Dominican Order and went to study at the College of San Gregorio at Valladolid.

Carranza was however a man of deep intellect and he was not one to curb his tongue. During his lectures he spoke more freely than was actually safe for any man, and he was not without his enemies.

Before he had passed his twenty-seventh birthday he could have been in serious trouble. A Dominican, one of the lecturers of the college, went to the Inquisition concerning Carranza and told the officials that his colleague harboured unhealthy notions. He had actually stated that the power of the Pope and Church were limited, and the only salvation was to be attained through Jesus Christ.

The Inquisitors considered this information and, for some reason known only to themselves, decided to do nothing about it. But such information was never lost; it was treasured, stored away in the archives for future reference.

Meanwhile another accuser appeared. This was a Dominican, Juan de Villamartin, who informed the Inquisition that Carranza was a great admirer of Erasmus and had often, in his lectures, defended those works of the scholar which had attacked confession and penance as ordained by the Catholic Church.

This was also docketed and put away.

Carranza began to climb to prominence. He was made a professor of Arts and junior professor of Theology, and in 1534 the great honour, not only of chief professor, but that of consulter of the tribunal of Valladolid was given to him. He even became Theologian Qualificator or Examiner of the Holy Office of the Inquisition of Valladolid, and in this role often acted.

In 1540 he was sent to Rome to represent his Order to the General Chapter, and there was given a doctorate by Paul III and with it a licence to examine and prohibit the introduction into Spain of heretical literature.

He was now well known through the country as a man destined for a very high place; and in 1542 was offered the See of Cuzco in the American Dependencies, but this he refused. In 1544 he was present on the first occasion when a Lutheran was burned. This was San Roman who died the martyr's death demanding of all those who watched him whether they did not envy him his happiness in dying for the true faith.

Perhaps Carranza never forgot this man.

He continued to rise. In 1545 the Emperor Charles selected him to go to the Council of Trent as one of the theologians, and while at Trent he showed himself to be the firmest possible supporter of the Catholic Church. At the same time however, he published a book – a very dangerous thing to do – the purpose of which was to reform the Bishops' custom of absenting themselves from their Sees, Carranza being assured that a Bishop could only do his best work if he lived in his diocese. This touched a lot of the Bishops in a vulnerable spot, and once again there was a flutter among Carranza's enemies. This time however they had grown in proportion to his fame. He was a very distinguished man and he had many enemies who would be only too eager at the appropriate moment to bring about his downfall.

In 1548 Charles offered him the post of confessor to Philip – one of tremendous influence, particularly with a man as religiously minded as Philip. Carranza refused this, as he did the See of the Canaries which was offered to him in 1550.

At that time he became Provincial of his Order in Castile and a year later was sent to join the Council of Trent, which had once again been convoked.

On returning to Spain he went back to San Gregorio at Valladolid. Meanwhile historical events were moving towards him.

Philip was about to contract a marriage with Mary Tudor, and he called upon Carranza to accompany him to England.

During the reign of Philip II the Inquisition grew to a new magnitude. Not one of Spain's monarchs was a more ardent supporter of this Institution than Philip, and there can be no doubt that it is due to his zeal that during his reign it came into its heyday.

Philip was every inch a Spaniard, as Charles, his father could never have been. Charles spent a very small proportion of his life in Spain and his sympathy and understanding always remained with the people of the Netherlands. He had been born in Flanders; he spoke the language of that country as he could never learn to speak Spanish; but it was more than a language which separated him from the people of Spain. He was German, and it is as the Emperor Charles V of Germany rather than Charles I of Spain that he is known.

How different it was with Philip! From that May day in 1527 when he was born in the Valladolid Palace he was a Spaniard and his upbringing accentuated this. He might have been named Philip after his grandfather Philip the Handsome, son of Emperor Maximilian, but there was little of the Hapsburg in this young man.

Philip was carefully instructed by his professors – Juan Martinez Siliceo to look after his academic life, and Juan de Zuñiga to teach him how to excel in sport. Zuñiga might be outspoken and not the man to mince his words even to the heir to the throne, but Siliceo was certainly not going to risk offending his pupil. It is typical of Philip's solemn nature that he was no more angered by Zuñiga's outspokenness than he was ready to take advantage of the accommodating nature of his professor.

It is clear that in Philip Spain was to have a very serious-minded King.

Philip was twelve years old when his mother died (1st May, 1539). The Emperor at this time was not quite forty, Isabella his wife was thirty-six. Charles however did not marry again. He was deeply engaged in wars away from Spain and he had his heir in Philip. Isabella had borne Charles two other sons but both of these had died of epilepsy when they were very young; and Philip, in spite of being small, seemed to be healthy. In any case there was no second marriage.

Charles was determined to train his son at a very early age for the greatness which was to come to him, for this pale-eyed boy would be heir to half the world one day.

When the boy was only sixteen Charles took him into his confidence with regard to his method of government; there were warnings to beware of the hypocrisy of statesmen, and Charles often discussed with his son the most important of these men, who would be Philip's advisers, dissecting their characters with a great deal of analytical skill, and some malice, for his son's enlightenment. In 1543 when Philip was but sixteen the Emperor left Spain, appointing Philip Regent during his absence. The Emperor could be sure that Philip would, no matter at what cost to himself, do his duty. Charles often wished that his son was a little gayer in personality, but he could not have had a more dutiful boy.

The royal families of Spain and Portugal had become closely related by continual intermarrying and, in November 1543, Philip married the Princess Maria of Portugal, his young cousin. She was five months younger than Philip and Philip was pleased with the match. He was not the kind of boy to have had a great deal to do with women and was prepared to be a good husband to little Maria.

Married life was short-lived however. In less than two years, on 8th July, 1545, Maria gave birth to a son. This was the notorious and ill-fated Don Carlos. Three days after the birth of Carlos, Maria died. Thus the young husband had become a young widower; it was true he had a son, but if he could have seen into the future he would have known that it would have been better to have no son rather than Carlos.

It was difficult for Charles to make the Flemings love his heir. The quiet, serious young man was so different from those noisy, pleasure-loving people, and so different from his father, that Charles often despaired of the relationship which must ensue between Philip and a very large proportion of his subjects.

Philip, of course, could not remain for ever unmarried, and the prospect of a bride for him occupied both the minds of himself and his father to a large extent.

There came the summer of 1553 and the death of Edward VI of England. Edward was succeeded by his half-sister Mary, daughter of Catalina of Aragon, aunt of the Emperor Charles. There seemed possibilities here of an alliance with England, for surely Mary, with her connections with the Spanish House, would be very ready to consider her Spanish kinsman with favour.

Moreover religious affairs had undergone a great change in England. Henry VIII had broken with the Pope and had abolished the monasteries. England had remained Catholic but not Papist. Yet during the reign of young King Edward VI there had been a welcome for the new Lutheran ideas in England and Protestantism became the recognized religion of the country.

Charles and Philip would say that fortunately the previous reign had been short, the King too young, for this to have had a great effect upon the people, and now on the throne was the daughter of their own Catalina of Aragon, as ardent a Catholic as her mother.

There is an interesting account of England of this day, which was given by the Venetian Giovanni Micheli. It was the custom of Venetian merchants at that time to visit foreign countries, assess their wealth and come back to their native Venice where they would read an account of their travels to the Doge and Senate.

London, declared Micheli, was one of the greatest cities in Europe and its population, including its suburbs, about one hundred and eighty thousand. England was strong enough to hold off any invasion in spite of a small navy; its army was strong, particularly in bowmen, in which art all Englishmen were trained from early days. There were no taxes on wine, beer and salt, nor on cloth – a great difference this, when compared with other countries in Europe whose people were crippled by taxation. The entire revenue was rarely more than two hundred thousand pounds. The royal will was law and rarely was the parliament summoned.

As for the Queen, she was thirty-six years of age and had been handsome in her youth. Unfortunately she suffered much from disease, and this had left its mark upon her countenance. She was clever, spoke many languages and was less frivolous than her half-sister Elizabeth. She was determined to bring the Catholic Faith back to England and had been heard to say that she would lose ten crowns rather than imperil her soul.

Mary, now that she was Queen of England, was turning her eyes towards Spain. When she had been a child of six, the Emperor Charles had visited England and had been persuaded by Mary's mother to enter into an agreement to marry the little girl. The disparity in their ages, however, was too great, and Charles too impatient a man to wait as long as he would have to wait for Mary.

Charles now determined to secure the English crown for Philip and accordingly wrote to Mary telling her that, since he himself had become infirm and elderly, he could not suggest marrying her himself. Therefore he offered her the person most dear to him: his son Philip.

After some coquetry on Mary's part the marriage treaty was drawn up.

This laid down that Philip should respect the existing laws and not interfere with the rights and liberties of Englishmen; that the power of conferring titles and offices, should remain with the Queen. Foreigners to the English were not to be given

140

office. If there should be male issue of the marriage, that son was to be heir to the English crown, and to Spanish possessions in the Low Countries and Burgundy. Should Don Carlos die, any son Philip should have by Mary should also inherit Spain and her dependencies. The Queen was not to be forced to leave England unless she desired to do so. If Mary should die, Philip was to claim no right in the government of the country.

In spite of this treaty, which was very favourable from the English point of view, there was a great outcry in London when its contents were made public; and there was much dissatisfaction throughout the country, the chief insurrection being that under the leadership of Sir Thomas Wyatt.

Meanwhile Philip made ready to leave Spain for England. The Regency was left in the hands of the Princess Juana, Philip's sister who was eight years his junior. Don Carlos, already showing himself to be a menace to his father's peace, was left in the charge of his preceptor, Luis de Vives.

Philip set sail for England on the 11th July, 1554, and with him were all the highest ranking gentlemen of the Castilian nobility – men such as Ruy Gomez the Prince of Eboli and the Duke of Alva. And as one of Philip's intentions while in England was to bring England back to the Church, with him sailed the man whom he and his father had considered the most suitable for this task: Bartolomé de Carranza.

Arrived in England Carranza became the associate of Cardinal Pole, and Philip let Mary know that he wished his Archbishop to be one of her chief advisers in her great task of re-establishing the Catholic Faith in her domain. Carranza was soon deeply resented by the English, who nicknamed him the Black Friar, partly because of his dark complexion and partly because of his Dominican robes.

Carranza, accustomed to the methods employed in Spain against heretics, was, according to many of his biographers, largely responsible for the Marian persecutions which culminated in the Smithfield fires. So unpopular did he become that several attempts were made on his life; he survived them all.

In September 1555, Philip, heartily tired of Mary and eager to escape from her cloying affection, joined his father in Flanders, However, he left Carranza in England, strongly advising Mary to keep him as her chief religious adviser; and Mary, who was eager to keep her husband's favour at all costs, agreed to do this.

When Mary came to the throne it was stated that 'Her Grace's conscience is stayed in the matter of religion, yet she meaneth graciously not to compel or strain other men's consciences otherwise than God shall (as she trusted) put in their hearts a persuasion of the truth that she is in, through the opening of His word unto them by godly virtuous and learned preachers.'

On the surface this sounds as though she intended to be lenient, but there is a hint of a threat in the words; she herself has the truth, she implies (always a dangerous assumption), and her learned preachers are going to put before her people the same truth.

Mary's true intention very soon became obvious. Certain laws which had been passed during the reign of her half-brother were repealed; one of these was the Act of Uniformity which allowed priests to marry. Those who had been teaching the Reformed Faith found themselves in prison – Latimer, Cranmer, Ridley and Hooper among them.

A petition had been drawn up, acknowledging the misconduct of England in breaking away from the Papal rule, and on the 30th November, 1554, with Mary and Philip on their knees in a ceremony which can only be called humiliating to the monarchy of England, that country was received back into the Apostolic fold.

In the following January (1555) a solemn procession took place in the streets of London to celebrate the re-conversion to Rome and the acceptance of the Pope's authority. This was led by the children of Grey Friars (Christ's Hospital) and of St Paul's schools; one hundred and sixty priests carried ninety crosses singing the Roman service as they walked. Eight Bishops were in the parade, with them Bonner himself, now come into his own after his years in the wilderness. In the streets that night there were bonfires; it was not very long before the people of London were to see bonfires of another nature.

The first court which was set up to deal with heresy was in the church of St Mary Overy, presided over by Gardiner, Bonner, Tonstal and three priests.

Hooper was brought before this tribunal after having withstood eighteen months imprisonment in the filthy Fleet Prison. Another, one John Rogers, who was Canon of St Paul's, stood on trial with him. Rogers had done a great deal of work on translating the Bible into English and was thus, in the opinion of men such as Bonner and Gardiner, guilty of heresy. He was a very bold man and when he was condemned, for he refused to recant, he asked that he might take a last farewell of his wife and children. Since he was a priest, Gardiner retorted, he had no wife, and then this self-righteous man went on to refer to Mrs Rogers and the children in the coarsest possible terms.

For six days Rogers and Hooper were kept in Newgate, and at the end of that time Rogers was taken to Smithfield. In the crowds he saw his wife with their children (eleven of them – and one a baby in arms) waiting for a last glimpse of him. He did not falter and when he was offered a pardon if he would accept the Catholic Faith, he answered that what he had preached he would seal with his blood. 'Thou art a heretic', the sheriff told him, to which Rogers replied: 'That will be known when the last day comes.' 'I will never pray for you,' the sheriff said. 'But I will pray for you,' replied Rogers. And when the fires were lighted he appeared to bathe his body in them most joyfully.

Hooper was taken to Gloucester and burned near the Cathedral. He too was offered pardon if he would recant; and he too refused it. He suffered dreadfully, for the faggots were sparse and green and would not burn easily and the fire only reached the lower part of his body because of the direction in which the wind blew. He called for more and more fire, and at length gunpowder was brought. He suffered the most acute agony for three quarters of an hour, and it is recorded that in the crowds who watched him die, there was much weeping and lamentation.

It is gratifying to note that the spectators of these scenes in England were very different from those blood-crazed fanatics of the *quemadero*.

Philip was wise enough to realize that the English did not take as naturally to this sport of burning heretics as did his own people, and it was he who suggested that they should not offer too many such spectacles to the people of England. The day after the burning of Hooper he caused a sermon to be preached in which the practice of burning heretics alive was condemned. But the lull was short-lived. After five weeks a weaver was burned in Smithfield, and a short while after others followed.

Mary by this time was experiencing one of those distressing false pregnancies, and she believed that the more heretics she burned the more likely God would be to make her fruitful! Therefore she was eager to continue with the persecutions.

Latimer and Ridley were burned. Latimer was fortunate – he died quickly – but Ridley suffered acutely for, as in the case of Hooper, he was not given enough faggots and one of his legs was completely destroyed by the fire before the rest of his body was touched.

Cranmer met his death in 1556, and before he went to the stake refused to recant and told of the shame he felt because, in his fear of death he had committed the ignominious action of signing a recantation. He thereupon renounced the Pope and the Catholic Church and when he was at the stake, we are told, he was seen to hold in the flames to be first consumed that right hand which had signed the recantation.

It is impossible to state with accuracy the numbers who, during the Marian persecutions, died by fire, torture or through being shut away in insanitary prisons.

There is the usual wrangling between Catholic and Protestant recorders when it comes to figures. Catholics declare that many of the victims were condemned as traitors and not for their religious beliefs. Protestants on the other hand are inclined to swell the numbers of martyrs.

One estimate is that of Dr Lingard, which is: 'in the space of four years almost two hundred people perished in the flames for their religious opinions'.

Maitland in his *Essays on the Reformation* gives the number as two hundred and seventy-seven, but some omissions from his list have been discovered. The total number must have been somewhere in the region of three hundred.

This is horrifying, yet, after a consideration of the Spanish Inquisition, it seems almost insignificant. It is interesting to note that there were very few persecutions in the north of England, probably due to the fact that the northern dioceses were far from the seat of government. London had the largest number, forty-three people having met their deaths at Smithfield; at Canterbury forty-one died; Colchester had twenty-three. But apart from those burned at the stake many died in prison and many were tortured to death; and although these figures may seem comparatively small, this period was one of the darkest through which our country has ever passed; the reason is that, owing to the Spanish marriage, for a few years our skies were darkened by the shadow of the Inquisition. Had Mary lived there is no doubt that Philip would have induced her to set up the Inquisition in this country, and that Mary herself would have been delighted to do so. Whether or not the people would have stood quietly by and allowed this to happen is a matter for conjecture.

I like to think that it could not have happened here, that the less excitable English, the less fanatical English, would never have allowed their fellow countrymen to be persecuted as were the inhabitants of Spain.

It is a fact that they did not gather in their thousands to watch a burning; they did not make a festival of it; the spirit shown at the Smithfield fires and those of Canterbury, Coventry, Lewes and other places was in no way similar to that at the *autos de fé* of Seville and Valladolid. The Spaniards willingly chanted their oath of allegiance to the Inquisition; they shouted abuse at the victims; they applauded their soldiers who ran their halberds through bodies already broken by torture, destined for the fire. But the English sullenly watched the fires;

and in later years when the cry of 'No Popery' echoed through the land, they showed they had not forgotten.

It was Carranza's boast that during the three years he was in England he had either burned, brought back to the Church or driven out of the country thirty thousand heretics.

Perhaps his zeal caused him to exaggerate a little; however, the fact remains that he played a large part in the Marian persecutions.

While he was in England Carranza had, by order of Cardinal Pole, who was the Papal Legate, helped the Queen in establishing the Catholic religion in the Universities and had drawn up the canons which were to be passed in a National Council. He had been particularly active in the condemnation of Thomas Cranmer; and in 1557 he joined Philip in Flanders to report on what was happening in England. While he was in Flanders he was still burning with fanatical zeal against heretics and seized a large number of books to which he gave a ceremonial burning.

When the Archbishop of Toledo died Philip decided to honour Carranza by bestowing this office upon him. It was the highest honour of the Church and with it went the Primacy of Spain. Carranza was not eager to accept. He had written a book, which was being printed in Antwerp, and this seemed of greater importance to him than any honour; as it turned out it was certainly to be so, but not in the way Carranza had hoped.

Philip however insisted on his accepting the Archbishopric, and Pope Paul IV during Carranza's preconisation in Rome dispensed with many of the usual formalities which involved an examination of the past life of the man under review, for he said Carranza was well known to him as a man devoted to the Catholic Church and one who had done it good service in England and Flanders as well as Spain.

Carranza was now at the height of his power; and his enemies had been increasing with the years. There were many who remembered how, at the Council of Trent, he had spoken against Bishops who did not live in their dioceses, and had even published a treatise on this subject. These envious people gathered together and discussed the rise of Carranza, asking one another whether there had not in the past been certain heretical statements attributed to him.

One of Carranza's foremost enemies was the Inquisitor-General Valdés. As Archbishop of Toledo, Carranza was beyond his control, for Carranza was supreme in the Church in Spain and if Valdés wished to arrest him on a charge of heresy he could not do so without the consent of the Pope.

Philip sent Carranza to Yuste to consult Charles on certain matters and when the Archbishop arrived at the Emperor's retreat he found Charles very weak indeed.

During his stay at Yuste Charles sought religious comfort from the Archbishop, and Carranza, who had recently come from countries such as England and Flanders where the Reformed religion was the accepted one, seems to have used expressions which were used in that Faith. His enemies were on the watch for every word he uttered, every gesture he made.

Juan de Regla who was the Emperor's confessor was very jealous because his master had chosen to turn to the Archbishop for comfort, and when at this bedside Carranza read a psalm and followed it with the words: 'Your Majesty may have full confidence; for there is not, nor hath been, any sin which the blood of Jesus hath not sufficed to efface,' these words were construed as being the expression of reformed thought and were remembered against him. Charles died and Carranza's methods of administering the last rites were noted and criticized.

Regla, Valdés, Melchor Cano, and Pedro de Castro, the Bishop of Cuenca, were all on the watch now. It was not usually difficult for the Inquisition to substantiate a charge of heresy when it decided to bring one.

The great chance came with the publication of Carranza's book *Commentaries on the Christian Catechism*.

Valdés bought a large number of copies of the book which he distributed with the instructions that a thorough search was to be made with a view to discovering heretical phrases. If anything were discovered, there must for a time be secrecy, but thorough notes should be made and kept.

It was at this time that the prisons of the Inquisition were filling with the Lutherans of Valladolid and Seville. If Valdés needed evidence against any man in Spain he had so many victims in his power that it was almost certain he could find what he wanted. These poor men and women had only to be taken to the torture chambers and put on the hoist or the rack where physical sufferings were so intense that they were ready to do or say anything that was required to buy a little respite from pain.

Thus from the torture chambers came further damning evidence against Archbishop Carranza.

There was one thing Valdés could do, and that was apply to the Pope telling him that Carranza was vehemently suspected of heresy, and to ask for permission to place him in the hands of the Inquisition.

The Dean of Oviedo, who was a nephew of Valdés was sent to the Pope to obtain the desired permission. The Pope had been a friend of Carranza's; he disliked the Spaniards and had referred to them as the scum of the Earth, adding that although they were now in possession of certain parts of Italy, a short while before they had been known in that country only as cooks. Even so, he was not eager to run into any trouble by defending Carranza, and all he did was delay matters a little.

Meanwhile news reached Carranza that his book was under suspicion. This aroused his alarm, which was indeed natural, and he wrote to Sancho López de Otalora who was a member of the Supreme Council that he was prepared to withdraw the book. If Valdés had really been concerned with preventing the spread of possible heresy this action of Carranza's should have satisfied him; but Valdés great desire was to make Carranza a prisoner of the Inquisition and to bring about his disgrace and downfall.

Meanwhile Paul IV died and Pius IV was elected; the latter confirmed the necessary permission, and Dean Valdés of Oviedo returned to Inquisitor Valdés in triumph.

When Philip heard that the man, whom he and his father had chosen to honour, was to be arrested on a charge of suspected heresy and brought before the Inquisition, he did nothing to save him. Philip had proved himself to be quite without sentiment even towards those who thought themselves to be his friends; and any lapse into heresy was in his eyes the greatest of sins. He was told that in addition to the suspicion attached to Carranza's works, many of the imprisoned Lutherans of Valladolid and Seville had testified against him. All Philip asked was that, since Carranza was Archbishop of Toledo and Primate of Spain, his arrest should take place without disturbing his dignity.

He then wrote to his sister Juana, who was once more Governess of Spain during his absence from the country, and told her that he wished her to summon Carranza to Court on some pretext; that when he was there he might, with the utmost decorum, be taken into custody.

The Princess accordingly wrote to the Archbishop telling him that he must come with all speed to Valladolid where he was summoned to wait the return to Spain of His Majesty the King.

This message was conveyed to him by Rodrigo de Castro who was a brother of Pedro de Castro, a man who had determined on Carranza's downfall; he was so eager to see Carranza arrested that he carried the message to Carranza's palace at Alcalá de Henares with such speed that when he arrived he was quite exhausted and had to rest a few days before he was able to go on.

Carranza was completely duped by the summons, and immediately arranged for special prayers to be said for the safe arrival of the King; at the same time he must have remembered the suspicions which his book had aroused, and he arranged not to leave until de Castro was sufficiently recovered to accompany him.

A few days after the arrival of de Castro, another visitor appeared. This was Diego Ramírez who had come to announce an Edict of Faith.

The proclamation was celebrated in the Church of San Francisco, and Carranza himself preached the sermon, telling the people that they must obey the Edict and, if they suspected any person of heresy, they must come forward and denounce that person.

It was noted that in the Edict there was on this occasion no mention of heresy in books; and this had probably been eliminated out of respect for the Archbishop.

Carranza was no doubt beginning to grow uneasy. From the moment his book had been under suspicion he could not have felt free from apprehension; he as much as anyone knew the methods of the Inquisition; he probably guessed that it was solely because of his position that he had been allowed to remain a free man.

He now seemed eager to delay the departure to Valladolid. He probably felt that if he could wait until Philip was in Spain he would have the support of a man on whose justice he could rely. He therefore, before leaving Alcalá, arranged to hold confirmations at various places through which he was to pass, so great was his desire to postpone the arrival at his destination.

At Fuente del Saz a monk, who was a professor of a college of Alcalá, came to Carranza and told him that rumours were circulating in Valladolid that there was a plot to arrest him and take him before the tribunal of the Inquisition; this monk advised him to return at once to Alcalá or to make with all speed to Valladolid, for in the quiet little villages on the road between these two places it would be a simple matter for the *alguazils* to descend upon him by stealth one night and carry him off to prison and he might never be seen again.

Carranza replied to this that his friend had been listening to wild stories. He had been summoned to Valladolid by the Princess Juana to await the King who was on his way home. How could he be under suspicion of heresy? Had he not recently come from England where he had led the campaign against heretics?

Valdés was eager to make the arrest. He was afraid that Carranza would reach Valladolid and that Philip himself might arrive there. If Carranza had a chance of putting his case before the King it was quite possible that he would free himself from suspicion. Valdés was determined that Carranza must not have that opportunity.

When Carranza reached Torrelaguna on Sunday, 20th August, 1559, there waiting for him was Fray Pedro de Soto who was full of dire warnings. Carranza was in imminent danger, he warned, for his friend, Luis de la Croz, had already been arrested in Valladolid. Carranza asked on what charge, and when told he replied: 'Then accordingly, they will make me a heretic!'

Disaster was nearer than he realized. The *alguazils* were gathering in stealth in Torrelaguna. Cebrian, chief *alguazil* of the Council of the Inquisition, was in one of the hostels of the town, staying in bed by day and emerging only at night, that his presence might not be suspected. On Tuesday, the 22nd, a hundred men were stationed within a short distance of Torrelaguna ready to close in for the arrest.

On Sunday, the 27th, Rodrigo de Castro took supper with the Archbishop; then, declaring that he was very tired, he left him and went to the house in which he was staying to make sure that his assistants were in readiness. He then returned to the house in which the Archbishop was lodging, and seeking out the landlord told him that he was about to give orders in the name of the Holy Office which must be obeyed to the letter. The trembling landlord readily assured de Castro that he, like all subjects of the King, was the willing slave of the Inquisition. That was good; he was to leave all the doors of his house unbarred that night.

During the night de Castro with several assistants entered the house in which the Archbishop lay and mounted the stairs, pausing outside that ante-room where the friar who served Carranza was sleeping. They knocked on the door. 'Who calls?' asked the friar, starting up from his bed. 'Open to the Holy Office,' was the answer. It was the summons which none dared disobey.

The door was opened and they walked through the ante-room to that where the Archbishop lay. 'Who is there?' asked the Archbishop in alarm. There came the dreaded answer: 'The Holy Office.'

Rodrigo de Castro entered and called to the leading *alguazil* to do his duty. 'Most illustratious Señor,' said the *alguazil*, 'the Holy Office commands me to make you its prisoner.' He then read the order from the Inquisitor-General and the Council.

Carranza pointed out that even the Inquisitor-General had no power to arrest the Primate of Spain. Whereupon the brief from the Pope was produced; and thus Carranza knew that his doom had come upon him.

He was taken from the town by night, and all the inhabitants were warned that they were not to look from their windows until the dawn; nor must they leave their houses; and when the miserable cortège reached Valladolid, Carranza was lodged in the house of Pedro González de Leon just outside the walls of the city.

The arrest had been carried out in the utmost secrecy, and many were afraid to mention the Archbishop's name. Some were imprisoned for talking of him and suggesting that he had been taken by the Holy Office. The whole affair was, as it was meant to be, wrapped in that secrecy so beloved by the Inquisition.

Carranza was not treated as badly as most prisoners who came into the prisons of the Inquisition. According to Llorente he was allowed an attendant, Fray Alonso de Utrilla, and a page, Jorje Gómez Muñoz de Carracosa. The party of three were given two rooms; this might imply some comfort, but the windows were shuttered and all light and air kept out; and the trio was not allowed to move out of these rooms for any reason whatsoever. This meant that the stench became poisonous and the Archbishop very soon succumbed to an illness which brought him near to death. A doctor who was allowed to see him said that the windows must be opened from time to time, but the Supreme Council of the Inquisition would not allow this, though they agreed that a small grating in the door might remain open if a guard were posted outside.

He was put under the charge of Diego González, who was one of the Valladolid Inquisitors, a miserable man, delighting in contemplating the wretched squalor to which a man who had once borne the highest title in Spain was reduced. He did little to help him, suppressing Carranza's correspondence with the Suprema when he thought fit, spying on him and misconstruing his actions in his reports.

It was considered inadvisable to take Carranza to the head-quarters of the Inquisition to face his judges; therefore Valdés, with the Supreme Council, came to the Archbishop's prison; and here Carranza, with a great show of courage accused the Inquisitor-General of having brought him to this pass, not because he suspected him of heresy, but because he was envious of his rise to power. Carranza and his friends felt their only hope to be in having the case tried in Rome, and this was what they were working for. Pius IV however, who might have been a friend to Carranza, was very eager not to offend Philip, and here again was one of those controversies between sovereign and Pope when each was more concerned with political advantage than the justice of the case under review.

Philip, who was never quick to act, waited a year before selecting new judges; and all this time the Inquisition and Philip were enjoying the enormous wealth of the Archbishopric of Toledo, and poor Carranza was languishing in his noisome jail.

In March of 1561 Philip appointed Gaspar Zuñiga, Archbishop of Santiago, as chief judge – a man known to be hostile to Carranza. Carranza however was allowed to choose two lawyers to defend him, and he selected Martin de Azpilcueta and Alonso Delgado.

Thus, it was two years after Carranza's arrest that his trial began. Carranza announced that during his two years' imprisonment he had continually tried to discover the reason for his arrest. He should, of course, have realized that he was in the hands of the Inquisition and it was the rule of this institution that prisoners should be kept in the dark as to their sins.

He was presented with thirty-one articles, to each of which he was to give a spontaneous answer. He realized then that the Inquisitors had combed his past life, from the time when he was a boy, in an endeavour to discover anything he had said or written which could be construed as heresy.

Another year passed while his case was being considered. Pius IV fretted in Rome. It was an offence against the dignity of the Church, he declared, to keep the Archbishop of Toledo so long a prisoner. He demanded that, if they could not bring the case to an end in Spain, there was one course open to them: transfer it to Rome to be settled.

In the midst of the wrangle between Spain and Rome Pius IV died, and in January 1566 St Pius V was elected to the Papal chair.

St Pius V was a strong man. He was the son of an Italian peasant and was clearly a man of very exceptional ability to have arrived at the highest office in the Church from his humble beginnings. He was a man of great energy determined to persecute heretics with all his strength, but at the same time he deplored the subversive methods which had been employed to this end. He was disturbed by the prolongation of the trial of the Archbishop of Toledo, and no sooner had he attained his office than he demanded the removal of Valdés from the office of Grand Inquisitor and that Carranza should be sent to Rome there to be tried by a tribunal which the Pope himself would set up.

Valdés was naturally furious, not only at the thought of handing his enemy over to the Pope, but also that it should be suggested that he himself should be dismissed. He sought to persuade Philip to stand out against Pope Pius V as he had against Pius IV; but the fifth Pius was a strong man; and when Philip countered with his usual hesitancy the new Pope thundered back that excommunication awaited those who flouted Papal authority. Philip decided on obedience. Valdés was dismissed from his post, and Carranza was taken from those two foul rooms, where he had existed for seven years, and sent under guard to Carthagena.

The Archbishop, who had been a healthy man when he was arrested, was now unable to walk and had to be carried in a litter.

When he reached Carthagena he remained there for four months during which time the Inquisitors refused to hand over to the Papal nuncio those papers dealing with the case. But eventually he left Carthagena and in May 1567 arrived at Civita Vecchia. He reached Rome a few days later and there he was made a prisoner in Castel Sant' Angelo.

Though still a prisoner, he found his new lodging was quite different from the old one. Here he could take exercise and enjoy the beautiful views from the windows. His health began to improve a little.

But the Pope seemed in no greater hurry to settle the fate of this long-suffering man than had the Spaniards, for he decided that all the papers must first be translated into Italian – a task which took the whole of what was left of that year to perform.

Further delays occurred by the discovery that the Spanish Inquisitors had not handed over all the papers; these had to be acquired and translated. The works of Carranza which were under discussion must also be translated into Italian; a year slipped away.

The Pope had set up a committee of seventeen consulters, four of whom were Spaniards who had been trying the case in Spain; they met once a week with the Pope as President.

The Pope now prepared his verdict. He had found the accusations of Valdés not proven; he commanded that the book, the publication of which had started the trouble, was to be given back to Carranza that he might translate it into Latin and have an opportunity of explaining those passages which had caused all the concern.

Pius believed that Philip would be delighted with this verdict. He had misunderstood Philip's true motives. Philip was filled with cold fury. He considered it an insult; as for the Inquisitors they too were incensed.

Unfortunately for Carranza, Pius V died (May 1572), only a few weeks after his ambassador arrived in Spain with the verdict, and Philip and the Inquisitors were ready to see in this death the hand of God which was, they believed, so firmly set against heretics.

They recorded their pleasure. The death of a man who had been willing to compromise the honour of the Spanish Inquisition for the sake of a Dominican monk could not be regarded as a great loss to Holy Church. On the other hand the death of such a Pope was a boon to the Inquisition.

The new Pope, Gregory XIII, was not such a bold man as his predecessor; he did not wish to antagonize a monarch of the stature of Philip II. Philip wished for the condemnation of Carranza in order to preserve what he considered to be the honour of Spain and the Inquisition. Gregory XIII was ready to do all in his power to oblige. He therefore took action against those bishops and theologians who had found no heresy in Carranza's works; they were threatened that they themselves might be suspected of heresy unless of course they were clever enough to discover new heresies in those written words.

In our period of partial freedom of speech, writing and the expression of opinion, it is easy to condemn these people, but one must remember that they had full knowledge not only of the terrible dungeons of the Inquisitions, those gloomy chambers of pain, but of the prolonged suffering of the Archbishop Carranza himself, if they had need to remind themselves of how the mighty could be brought low. One of these men was the Archbishop of Granada who was noted for his piety and would in a more lenient age have won great respect. But he was an old man; he could not be expected to view with equanimity all the horrors that the Inquisition was capable of forcing upon him. He was one of those, who, to save himself, discovered new heresies in the works of Carranza.

As a result, where sixty-eight of the propositions set out in Carranza's Catechism had been judged tainted with heresy, now there were two hundred and seventy-three.

Another two years passed and still the trial dragged on; and at length in April 1576 there assembled in the Hall of Constantine, the Pope, cardinals, prelates and counsellors to pronounce sentence. Carranza was brought before them.

Thus came this poor old man, quite devoid of all hope after seventeen years of imprisonment. He was now approaching seventy-three years of age, and when misfortune had first fallen upon him he had been but fifty-six. He came to stand before the Pope, bareheaded, bent double with infirmity, trembling with senility and certainly apprehension.

The Pope then announced that:

Carranza was vehemently suspected of certain errors and would be required to abjure them.

He was to be suspended and removed from the administration of his church for five years, and to await the pleasure of the Pope and the Holy See before he was allowed to regain any of his lost dignities.

During that time he was to retire to a monastery which had been chosen for him in Orvieto; and he must not leave this monastery without the consent of the Pope and the Holy See.

The Pope proposed to appoint an administrator of the church of Toledo; and all its riches accumulated since the day of the Archbishop's arrest and during his suspension, would be taken for the use of the Church, after the expenses such as pensions and debts had been dealt with.

A thousand crowns from this vast wealth should be set aside each month for the maintenance of the Archbishop.

Penances would be imposed upon him.

It was prohibited for any to possess, read or print his Catechism.

So ended the trial which had been prolonged for seventeen years.

The captain of the guard conducted Carranza to the Dominican monastery of Santa Maria sopra Minerva. The first of his penances was to visit seven churches on the Saturday of Easter week. Gregory, having passed the sentence to please Philip and the Spanish Inquisition then seemed to be worried by his conscience. He offered Carranza his own litter and horses. He also offered him a letter in which he set out his esteem for the ex-Archbishop and wrote of his concern for his future. Both these offers Carranza refused with the utmost dignity. However, he began his penance and visited the seven churches; and when he did so, the people turned out in crowds to follow him from church to church and show him the sympathy they felt for his sufferings, and their refusal to believe in his guilt: some consolation, though a poor one for the suffering of years.

In a few days he became very ill, and hearing of his plight Gregory immediately sent him absolution and exemption from further penances.

Knowing that his end could not be far off, Carranza sent for his secretaries and before them made a solemn declaration that he had never swerved from the true faith.

He died on 2nd May, 1576.

His death was considered a little mysterious and therefore an autopsy was ordered. Slight ulcers were discovered in the kidneys and gall-bladder, but there was no whisper that he had died of poison. His death, though, is not without suspicion. It may have been that the long arm of the Spanish Inquisition had caught him and hustled him to his death. His popularity as seen when he visited the seven churches must have been alarming to those who might have felt that his return to Toledo was not an impossibility.

However seventeen years of terrible uncertainty and horror, lived partly in noisome prisons, could easily have brought an old man to his death.

Philip would never have tolerated his return, and Gregory could have used Carranza in his intrigues against Spain. There would have been many people – Philip among them – who must have determined that Carranza must never return to Spain; and these people were such as did not hesitate to administer a dose of poison to those who stood in their way.

But if we are uncertain as to how Carranza died, we are by no means so concerning the long imprisonment; and his case is one of the most outstanding in the annals of the Inquisition because it gives us such an indication of what could happen to the highest in the land, not because of their religious opinions, but on account of envy.

It is hard to believe that any of Carranza's accusers ever thought him guilty of heresy. His zealous persecution of Cranmer and his kind in England showed him to be a staunch supporter of the Catholic Church. As for his writings, it is often possible to misconstrue words when the desire to do so is acute enough.

His case is so interesting because it showed how powerful was the Inquisition in Spain, how unwise and dangerous it was for a man to possess great wealth and standing, and so arouse the enmity of his fellows.

Carranza's story must have been a warning to every man in Spain. Now surely they must have realized the nature of this monster which they had nourished in their midst.

The terrible example of Carranza showed that in Spain no man, no matter how rich or influential he might be, was safe from the Spanish Inquisition.

CHAPTER TEN

WITCHCRAFT AND THE INQUISITION

I have often heard the opinion expressed by Catholics that the Inquisition was a necessity because witchcraft was growing at an alarming rate throughout Europe, and that the Holy Office was set up as a deterrent.

It is rather strange that this reason should be given, for those countries in which trials for witchcraft were predominant were not those where the Inquisition flourished; although it was one of the duties of Inquisitors to examine those suspected of witchcraft.

There is a widely held opinion that witchcraft was actually a relic of paganism. It was not a form of heresy, but had its very roots in the religion which had flourished before the spread of Christianity, and at the Sabbats – those weird midnight gatherings to which witches were supposed to ride on their broomsticks, taking with them their familiars, usually in the shape of cats – were practised the fertility rites.

The wild dances, performed in the nude, were calculated to stimulate sexual desire, a very understandable procedure when life was held cheap and it was advisable continually to replenish the population. At these ceremonies we hear of the presence of the Horned God, usually in the shape of a goat, who was supposed to be Satan; this horned creature usually selected the most desirable of the females for his mate during the orgy; and it is possible that he may have been the most enterprising member of the group who had disguised himself as a goat. All the ceremonies of the Sabbat, it seems, were calculated to produce sexual abandon; for instance the nature of the dances, the abandoning of clothes, and the sign of allegiance to the Horned God which was to kiss him beneath his tail.

It is no easy matter to supplant one religion by another. It appears that the new religion has been accepted; people are baptized, quote creeds, say prayers and declare themselves believers, but old superstitions cling.

Christianity appeared to have been accepted, but men still worshipped the sun and trees; they still clung to the old charms which would provide lovers, babies, good fortune for themselves and bad for their enemies.

According to the Venerable Bede, King Redwald who lived in the seventh century kept two altars in his temple; one to placate the Christian God, the other for the pagan gods. Clovis the King of the Franks, when attacking the Allemannians at Tolbiac, was contemplating becoming a Christian and offered to do so if the God of his Christian wife, Clotilde, would give him the victory; but he did not forget to pray to the old gods at the same time. Too much was at stake to risk offending any gods; and superstitious man could not imagine a god who had not all the pride, envy and vindictiveness of man himself.

Witchcraft comes to us from the Palaeolithic age and has stayed with us even until the present day. Some ten years ago a woman living in Cornwall visited a doctor friend of mine and, when all doors had been closed and certain precautions taken against the powers of witchcraft, she told him that her neighbour had 'overlooked her baby' and she feared the worst.

It is small wonder that in the thirteenth century such beliefs were rife and had a strong grip on a certain section of the population even as late as the nineteenth.

It was when a worship of the devil was discovered in witchcraft that it was seen as heresy, and then the Inquisition stepped in, in order to suppress it.

Those who were suspected of witchcraft often seemed to have had a great desire for confession and revelled in recounting the stories of their sins: they talked freely of their adventures at the Sabbats and of their familiars and devils with whom they enjoyed sexual intercourse. They seemed to suffer from hysteria and really believed the fantastic stories they told. Torture and hideous death was the lot of many; thousands were burned alive; and that death alone not being considered bad enough for them many suffered also by having their flesh first torn by red hot pincers; and the fires which burned them were slow fires. In France it was a custom to seize the children of witches, strip them and beat them with rods round the town while their parents were burned alive. One French commentator, himself a judge who had been guilty of passing this inhumane sentence on innocent children, deplored the fact that this was all that happened to them (except of course that they lived the rest of their lives under suspicion and were likely to be tried for witchcraft at any time).

In order to stamp out witchcraft the Church and State stood firmly together, and witches were judged by both episcopal and secular courts. In 1437 Eugenius IV was urging Inquisitors throughout Europe to display greater zeal in bringing witches to judgment.

With the appearance of Jacob Sprenger's *Malleus Maleficarum*, Hammer of Witches, in 1489, witchcraft increased. The publication of the book meant that people were more deeply aware of witchcraft and that many were eager to dabble in it; the authorities looked for witches and they were determined to find what they sought.

Jacob Sprenger was a fanatic; he had acted as Inquisitor in Germany where, Innocent VIII declared in his Bull of 1484, witches abounded and endeavoured to seduce the good people of those lands to follow their malignant lead.

There was a theory at this time that those who worked for the suppression of witchcraft were protected by God and could not be harmed by witches and their familiars, or the demons who were sent from hell to help them. A holy relic worn on the body served as protection, it was believed; and witches grew pale and fled if a victim made the sign of the cross in their presence. Sprenger declared that he and his colleagues, during witch-hunts, had often been confronted by devils in some animal form. They had never been harmed by them, however, because they were employed in God's service.

This, however, did not always appear to be effective for Sprenger states that witches often bewitched their judges while they were in the act of sentencing them; and during a burning in the Black Forest a witch, at the moment when her executioner was lighting the faggots at her feet, blew into his face telling him that he should be rewarded for what he had done that day. Immediately he was afflicted by leprosy and was dead within a few days, we are told.

Such stories inflamed the imagination, and as Sprenger's superstitious legends were accepted as truth, the whole world was ready to believe that witchcraft was the cult of the devil.

But, asked some, if God was all-powerful, how was it that the devil was able to give such power to his followers? The explanation was a rather feeble one. It was this: God sometimes allowed Satan a certain amount of power which enabled him to raise a storm or kill people and animals, but Satan could only work within the limits God allowed him. God sometimes allowed him to create illusions in which men believed. There were no such things as riding on broomsticks to Sabbats; this was all part of the illusions which God allowed the mischievous Satan to create; and incubi and succubi were unable to make children.

But the judgment was that witches, in worshipping Satan, committed heresy and should be put to death.

The more witchcraft was talked of, the more zealous the Inquisitors became in their endeavours to stamp it out.

Witches flourished in Germany and Italy in very large numbers, and in the hundred years or so which followed the fifteenth century the cult began to multiply alarmingly.

During the fifteenth century a witch was occasionally burned alive; later they were burned by the hundred. We hear that, in the town of Ravensburg at the end of the fifteenth century, forty-eight witches were burned in five years; there is an account from Geneva a few years later of five hundred burning in three months; and in Savoy eight hundred were condemned together.

In 1586 the winter was a very cold one on the banks of the Rhine, and the cold weather continued into the summer with lamentable results to the harvest. Because there was at this time a witchcraft craze in progress, witchcraft was judged to be the reason for the unusual weather. As a result one hundred and eighteen women and two men were imprisoned and hideously tortured until they confessed to having tampered with the elements; they were burned alive. And so extraordinary was the fascination of witchcraft that these people must have believed that they were responsible for the weather, since they declared even on their way to their deaths, that had they not been arrested they would have continued with their plots and all the corn would have been destroyed together with all the fruits.

It seems that a great deal of physical torture and even hideously prolonged death, were considered a fair price to pay for the assumed possession of such extraordinary powers.

One supporter of the Inquisition records that from the beginning of the fifteenth century and for the next hundred and fifty years the Inquisition burned at least thirty thousand witches; and thus the world must thank the Holy Office, for had these witches been allowed to live they would have destroyed the world.

One wonders what the people were expected to think of the all-powerful God, who was said to allow Satan his powers for some perverse and unaccountable reason.

So from the fifteenth to the nineteenth century there were outbreaks of witchcraft in Europe. The more it was talked of, the more persecutions there were. It appeared to have a fatal fascination for women more than for men; it is perhaps explained by the fact that these people were obsessed by the desire to call attention to themselves. Many of them were old, ugly, poor and of no account; and when they heard the constant talk of witchcraft and saw the fear it inspired in so many people, they must have realized that they too could acquire power over their fellow men and women; that it was power presumed to be derived from Satan, that it could bring them to hideous torture and death seemed of small account. When they became known as witches they acquired power, and their dull and very boring lives were lifted out of their monotony. There have always been people who are ready to risk their lives to escape from boredom.

In 1484 Innocent VIII put witches into a different category from that in which they had till this time existed, with his Bull

Summis desiderantes. Calixtus III, Pius II, Alexander VI, Julius II, Leo X, Adrian VI and Clement VII all lifted their voices against the cult and declared that it was the duty of the Church to exterminate witches.

Strangely enough there were fewer witches in Spain than in other European countries. This may have been due to the fact that the Spanish Inquisition acted against them, and there was a deep-rooted dread in Spain of falling into the hands of that secret organization which was so powerful that even the most sensation-crazy would-be witch would pause to consider before laying herself – or himself – open to prosecution.

Witchcraft had been prevalent in France, and that district of Spain which was most infected by the cult was the adjoining mountainous one of the Pyrenees.

One of the first cases of witchcraft dealt with by the Inquisition was that of Gracia la Valle who was burned alive in Saragossa in 1498.

There does not appear to be another case until 1499 when Maria Biesa was burned; and when one considers what was going on in other parts of Europe it seems that witchcraft had scarcely touched Spain. Llorente states that in the Biscay area more than thirty witches were burned in 1507; and there are accounts of rigorous efforts in 1517 against witches in Catalonia.

In 1522 an Edict of Grace was presented to all witches in the area of Jaca and Ribagorza. They were given six months in which to come forward and confess their sins. What is so extraordinary is that the Spanish Inquisition should show such leniency towards witches when in Northern Italy, where there seemed an unlimited supply of witches, they were being burned by the thousand.

Perhaps the answer is that the Spanish Inquisition was not entirely convinced that witchcraft was a heresy; many of the Inquisitors had insisted that it was impossible for women to fly through the air on broomsticks, and that those women who confessed that this was what they did were suffering from delusions. That these delusions were the result of communication with the devil they did not doubt, and they were of the opinion that any who had intercourse with the devil were only fit for the torture and the stake; but at the same time there was a divided opinion as regarded witches and this may have induced a certain leniency towards them. Another point – and perhaps this is the real reason – witches were for the most part poor old women with no possessions. One of the great incentives to prosecutions – as is seen in the case of Archbishop Carranza – was the hope of confiscating the wealth of the victim. Poor old women had nothing to bring to the coffers of the Inquisition. Was this the real reason why the Suprema was comparatively lenient towards them? And so perverse is human nature that the fewer prosecutions the less the interest in witchcraft; when interest was lacking, there was not the same urge among these poor women to tell fantastic stories about their adventures with the devil.

However in 1528 the Inquisitor-General, Alfonso Manrique, gave orders to one of his Inquisitors, Sancho de Carranza de Miranda, to make a very detailed enquiry into the spread of witchcraft in Calahorra and to punish any witches discovered with the utmost severity, for reports had reached him that the harvests were being affected to an alarming degree in that district, and that many young children had been killed. Even so Edicts of Grace were published and the Supreme Council urged caution and moderation, for it was so difficult to arrive at the truth in these cases of witchcraft where women, suspected of consorting with the Devil, only had to be brought before an examiner to indulge in the wildest aberrations which it was felt could not be true.

Moreover Inquisitors were told that they must verify the truth of accusations before making arrests. Such leniency is hardly credible. How different the treatment of witches from that of *Marranos, Moriscos* and Lutherans. Surely this lukewarm attitude *must* have had its roots in the small amount of profit to be obtained from persecuting witches.

When there was a scare in Navarre in the year 1538, Inquisitor Valdeolitas was sent to investigate, but his instructions were to ignore the hysterical demands of the population and make certain, before he arrested a single witch, that he had good reason for doing so. He was to explain to the people that bad harvests came in places where there were no witches and were not necessarily the result of the powers given by Satan to evil women.

An example of the Inquisitorial attitude is given in the case of Anastasia Soriana, the twenty-eight-year-old wife of a peasant, who presented herself before the tribunal which had been set up at Murcia and declared that she had had a carnal relationship with a devil. She was told to go home as she was suffering from delusions.

Where else but in Spain could this have happened in the year 1584?

But the woman was obsessed by the idea. Clearly she wished to be the paramour of a demon, for she presented herself once more to the tribunal – this time at Toledo – and told the same story. Once again she was told she was suffering from delusions and sent home.

In 1591 three women were arrested in Cazar. These were Catalina Matheo, Joanna Izquierda and Olalla Sobrina. It appeared that the deaths of several children had occurred in their village; the women were tortured, and under torture Catalina made a confession.

She said that Olalla had come to her some years before and talked of the delights of sexual intercourse with demons. Would Catalina like to be provided with a demon-lover? Catalina was fascinated by the idea, and one night she was asked by the third woman, Joanna Izquierda, to visit her house. When she arrived, Olalla was present and they had not been there very long when an extraordinary being arrived in the form of a goat. They stripped and danced with the goat until they were roused to a frenzy; the orgy continued far into the night and Catalina was introduced to the delights of intercourse with a demon. Later, for a little diversion – so said Catalina – they left the house and flew through the night to the home of a newly born infant. This they suffocated; and afterwards they all flew back again.

Olalla when tortured told nothing however, and when Catalina's story was put to her she emphatically denied it. Joanna also withstood torture, but she could not resist boasting of her exploits to the wife of her jailor.

She told this woman that witches and demons had come to her house and, after anointing her body, carried her to a Sabbat by force. There were generally assumed to be two ways of attending a Sabbat: one was by flying there, usually on a broomstick; the other by anointing the body with oil and rubbing it in until a stupor was produced; then the anointed one was conveyed there by supernatural forces. When she reached the Sabbat, Joanna told the jailor's wife, she had seen Olalla and Catalina there; they had all kissed the Horned God under the tail, danced the wild dances and indulged in the orgy which followed.

When the women were taken before the Tribunal of the Inquisition, Catalina admitted that what she had said was false; she declared that she had said it on account of the severity of the torture. Neither Joanna nor Olalla broke down under the further torture which they had to endure.

These women really escaped very lightly. Catalina, who had confessed (that she had done so under torture was ignored), had to appear at an *auto de fé* where she received two hundred lashes. The other two women merely appeared at the *auto* to make their confessions; and no further penance was imposed upon them.

It is safe to say that only in Spain and in no other country in the world at this time would these women have escaped so lightly. It is almost certain that anywhere else they would have been hanged or burned alive, and that witch hunts would have been started as always happened after a burning. People would believe when misfortune overtook them that witchcraft was working against them and would seek to find the witches. As a result of this leniency which took place in 1591, there were no more cases of witchcraft in the area for almost twenty years.

The Supreme Council of the Inquisition most certainly protected many people from charges of witchcraft. The people and the secular courts would have liked to see more witchcraft trials. They provided an entertainment, and from time to time many sought to work up a scare. The orgies which were reputed to take place at the Sabbats were discussed at great length; no abomination was too vile to be suggested. Sexual adventure was of course the most discussed – the prowess of the Devil himself and the succubi and incubi he provided for those who were faithful to him. That was not all. Witches were said to dig up corpses and eat them at their Sabbat feasts. They were reputed to find the blood of children very delectable; and the bones of new-born infants were needed for their spells and potions.

Yet the Suprema insisted that it was easy to be deceived by charges of witchcraft, and all information, it was decided, should be sent to the Council for investigation. In 1555 when many people were arrested on suspicion of witchcraft in the Guipúzcoa area, the Suprema reproved the tribunal and expressed fear that many innocent people might be involved. An order was issued that no more arrests were to be made without first submitting all details to the Suprema.

In this tale of terrible suffering which the Inquisition brought to Spain it is very pleasant to be able to record something in its favour; and perhaps it is rather churlish to look for the motives which prompted such action. Let it be said however that the action of the Inquisition in Spain towards witchcraft was such that it stopped the development of the cult which spread throughout the rest of Europe. By refusing to take witchcraft seriously, the Inquisition destroyed the desire of many people to indulge in it. Consequently Spain remained comparatively free from witchcraft and all its attendant horrors which prevailed in Europe from the fifteenth to the nineteenth century.

Even in Britain – usually so much more moderate than other European countries – the total number of witches done to death is in the neighbourhood of thirty thousand (at least a quarter of this number were executed in Scotland).

Here then is some good performed by the Inquisition; a very small credit to set in the balance sheet against the overwhelming evil – but still, it is something, and there is no doubt that many old women in Spain avoided torture and hideous death because of the existence of the Spanish Inquisition.

CHAPTER ELEVEN

MYSTICS AND THE INQUISITION

It was inevitable that this race of Spaniards, made up of Iberians, Tartesians, Phoenicians, Romans, Visigoths, Arabs and others, should be possessed of a strong streak of mysticism.

With the setting up of the Inquisition and the expulsion of first the Jews then the Moors, there was born in the people a religious fervour. The Inquisition had taught them that it was their duty to spy for the sake of the Church. It was more than a duty: It was a sin not to report any enemy of the Church.

Periodically these people saw the green cross, draped in black, carried in solemn procession to the city squares; they heard the bells of the prisons tolling and saw the prisoners, arrayed in hideous *sanbenitos*, emerge; they saw men and women who had been tortured so cruelly that they could not stand and had to be carried to the place of execution; they saw the penances which were imposed; men and women whipped through the streets; and they saw the faggots lighted at the feet of living men and women.

All this was treated as though it were a sacred duty – a ceremony for Sundays and Saints-days. It was not to be wondered at that in such a country there should be an emotional uprising, a preoccupation with mysticism.

As there were those who professed to be witches in league with the Devil, there were those who declared themselves to be singularly blessed to have communication with Christ or the Virgin Mary. These people ran a risk of being proved impostors; but like the witches, they found the temporary glory of setting themselves apart from their fellow men well worth the risk.

Hence throughout Spain there appeared many *beatas* or devout women, all of whom claimed to have been sanctified in some way. They were admired and respected by the population, who were ready to believe in them. Even a man as intellectual as Cardinal Ximenes himself was ready to accept certain *beatas* as holy women, as he showed when he turned back from a visit to Gibraltar on the advice of one, and by his support of the *Beata* of Piedrahita.

After the death of Santa Teresa many wished to follow her example, but there was a time during the life of this saint when she was in danger of being accused as an impostor.

People believed that they could attain the desired state by submitting the body to privations and thus subduing the flesh and increasing the power of the spirit. Devotees of this cult tried to deprive themselves of sleep and even whipped themselves, inflicting painful wounds in order to keep themselves awake. Hair shirts were common and the wearing of them taken as a matter of course. It is almost certain that these people were in a state bordering on hysteria; sleepless, half starved, they would be a prey to delusions; and it is very possible that many of them believed the fantastic stories of their adventures which they told were true.

Santa Teresa explains her union with God by saying it was a form of ecstasy or trance, during which the soul leaves the body.

'I do not see God with the eyes of my soul,' she writes, 'yet I know Him with a strange certainty.'

She tells us that at Easter 1579, at the time when she was founding the Barefooted Carmelities, she was uncertain concerning this new order and prayed for guidance; the result was a vision of Christ who gave her what she needed.

When Teresa died one of her followers, Catalina de Jesus, declared that she had visions of Teresa who told her what to do with regard to the Order; this was bound to lead to difficulties, for when another of Teresa's followers wished to work along different lines it was easy for her to have – or imagine she had – a vision of Teresa confirming what *she* wished.

Mysticism was clearly a dangerous weapon in the hands of those who were not necessarily unscrupulous but merely hysterical. When conversations with Christ and the Virgin Mary were not considered an impossibility, what a simple matter it was for some highly strung man or woman, whose body had not only been ill-nourished but tormented, to imagine that he was admitted to one of these conversations! And how simple for those who were entirely unscrupulous to invent fantastic adventures with the Deity, to pass on 'His Orders' and thus get what was wanted.

Zapata gives an indication of how easy it was at this time to dupe the people. The story he tells is of a company of travellers who moved about the country, stopping at various inns during their journey.

There were thirteen of these men – a significant number – and it was their custom to arrive at an inn where one of the thirteen would approach the innkeeper and tell him that he was greatly honoured, for his guests that night were Christ and his twelve disciples.

The innkeeper, superstitious, his mind full of the wonderful adventures of the *beatas* and saints, would believe what he was told.

He would call to his staff to produce a meal – a meal such as they had never produced before; bowls of water would be brought out that the feet of 'Christ' and the 'disciples' might be washed.

The company would accept the attentions, allow their feet to be washed, and would partake of the supper; then one of the 'disciples' would summon the innkeeper to the table and tell him that Christ asked that he should confess his sins. The poor innkeeper would probably fall on his knees, remembering all the little sins he had committed (usually cheating his customers), really believing that the silent man at the head of the table to whom the rest of the company showed such veneration, was Christ and therefore was aware of every little squalid act.

After the confession judgment would be passed. The innkeeper would be told to bring out all the money he possessed, and warned that it would be dangerous to hold any back for he was in the presence of the Omnipotent, Omniscient Being. When the money was brought forth it would be divided into portions. There would be a little for the innkeeper, that portion which had been, according to the 'disciples', honestly earned. A certain amount would also go back to the innkeeper to pay for the supper just eaten; it was tainted money, pointed out the 'disciples', but the fact that it had bought a supper for 'Christ' removed the taint. As for the rest of it – the far larger part – that was to go where it belonged – to the devil.

The charade was well staged, for at that precise moment the door of the inn would open and in would come a figure wearing horns and hoofs.

'Take your own!' the 'disciples' would cry; and 'Satan' would swoop on the money and disappear with it.

It was an interesting and well thought out little scene, with 'Christ' and the 'disciples' appearing to take nothing for themselves; of course when they left the inn they caught up with 'Satan' and there was a general share-out.

The little act went on for some time, the simple country people believing in it. Eventually some bold spirit declared himself dissatisfied and asked that the company of fourteen be arrested at that moment when 'Satan' flew in to take the money.

Thus a discomfited master, his band of disciples and the visiting Satan were all taken before the authorities. Satan shorn of horns and hoofs proved to be an ordinary man, and the identity of the remaining thirteen was soon established.

The result: fourteen criminals were publicly whipped and sent to the galleys. (From *Miscelánea de Zapata*.)

But that such a fraud could have taken place is an indication of the receptive state of mind of the people of Spain at this time.

Mysticism did not give the Church any great cause for anxiety until the coming of Lutheranism. To watch a great split in the Christian Church and to see another Church spring up to exist side by side with the Catholic one, a Church which threatened to become equally powerful, filled all serious-minded Catholics with alarm. They must be on the alert for all who diverged from orthodox thought. Thus they turned their attention to the mystics.

The task before the Inquisition was an extremely difficult

one. Mystics declared that they committed no sin against the Church; they lived holy lives and it was thus they obtained their communion with God, the Father, Son, Holy Ghost and the Virgin Mary.

The Inquisition realized that if they accused these people and brought them before their tribunals they could bring ridicule upon themselves, for mystics of the past had been canonized.

But many mystics were straining away from the orthodox Church and thus in this age of Reformation, they were becoming highly dangerous. Those who diverged from orthodoxy were known as *Alumbrados* (the Spanish version of the Italian *Illuminati*) and it was the Inquisition's duty to suppress them, at the same time employing the greatest caution. The fact that many of the mystics were impostors (*Embusteros*) was helpful.

What the Inquisition was compelled to do was differentiate between the orthodox mystic (who could do no harm and might eventually become a saint) and the *Alumbrado*, who either sought or was suspected of seeking to introduce new ideas which, because of this person's holy reputation (she or he having been believed to be in communication with the saints and the Deity and thus having the information straight from the source of all wisdom), might have an alarming effect on a great number of people.

Edicts of Faith began to be issued which were to lead to the detection of *Alumbrados*.

Their sin was that they preached the all-importance of mental prayer and the uselessness of oral prayer, and that those who wished to aspire to holiness should do nothing but meditate on holiness. They were reputed to speak against marriage and to declare that only their particular sect was the right one (one would have thought this failing common enough among all sects and unnecessary to be stated). They went into trances and declared that this was the outward sign of their state of grace, and that they possessed the Holy Ghost. They declared that there was no need for those who had reached this state of spiritual glory to close his or her eyes at the elevation of the Host or even to reverence images and listen to sermons.

All this was error in the eyes of the Church for these people were flagrantly denying certain laws laid down by the Church. Thus they were guilty of heresy, and it was the duty of the Inquisition to extirpate heretics.

One of the most well-known *beatas* and one whose case gives a very good example of the working of the Inquisition in this field, is that of Francisca Hernandez.

Francisca was undoubtedly an individualist; she wished for all the honour and prestige which came the way of holy women, but she was not very keen on suffering all the privations which were usually necessary to call attention to a state of holiness.

It is a tribute at least to her originality that she managed to attract attention without these practices.

She did not enter one of the religious orders – as so many did who had gone before and were to come after her; she did not wear the unbecoming habit of a nun; she lived in comfort in a house provided for her by her followers; and she had two maids to look after her comforts. She was visited by many admirers of her holiness, and she had a preference for masculine admirers; her bed was reputed to be a soft one and she did not always sleep in it alone; and far from starving herself she was very fond of her food, and there is a story that she once, in an unholy outburst, slapped the face of one of her maids because she had overcooked the dinner.

She was illiterate, but it was said that she was capable of performing miracles; people believed that she had the power of healing; and articles which had been in her possession were eagerly sought by her followers as holy relics.

The attention of the Inquisition was turned upon her, and she was brought up for questioning. The Inquisitor-General – at that time Adrian of Utrecht, for it must have been about 1518 – himself saw her. Judging a *beata* was a very delicate matter. If she were condemned, her followers would be enraged, and these women always seemed to inspire their followers with great devotion; on the other hand she might be proved to be sincere; *beatas* and holy women of the past who had had strange visions and performed miracles had been canonized. Adrian was an ambitious man; he had no wish to put it on record that he had condemned a woman who subsequently became a saint.

Therefore he acted warily. He decided that Francisca should not be punished in any way. He also had to consider however the possibility that later she might be proved to be an impostor. In that case he would not wish it to be said that she had been brought before him and he had found her innocent.

A very difficult position! Adrian therefore ordered that although she was discharged, a watch should be kept on her by the Inquisition.

Francisca must have been a very clever woman, for she certainly impressed Adrian. When he was elected Pope Adrian VI in 1522, he remembered Francisca and asked for her intercession with God and the saints for himself and the Church.

For some years after her first encounter with the Inquisition Francisca was left in peace, living in her comfortable house, waited on by her maids, receiving her masculine admirers, performing her miracles and so on.

She was undoubtedly a very fascinating woman and a very handsome one; and among the men who admired her so ardently was a certain Francisco Ortiz.

Ortiz was of the Franciscan Order, a young man who had already made his mark as a great preacher. The Order expected great things from him and there was enthusiastic interest in his career.

He had heard of Francisca and was very eager to meet her. He was nineteen years old when he endeavoured to bring about this meeting but it did not take place until six years later. He, being a friar, could not visit a woman without the consent of his Superior, and this was denied him.

This was the year 1523, and by that time his reputation had grown. Charles the Emperor had shown a special interest in him for when he was speaking the churches were full. There were some of course to listen suspiciously to what this young man said; every preacher of brilliance must encounter a certain amount of suspicion, for after all when so many people flocked to hear him, his influence was great. Never had the Catholic

Church felt itself to be in such jeopardy as it was at this time, with the Reformation breaking out all over Europe.

Charles however was so impressed by the young man's ability that he offered him the post of Court preacher. Although Francisco Ortiz had not met Francisca Hernandez there had been communication between them; and before he accepted a post of such eminence he asked her advice. She warned him against it, and because of this he refused it.

The fact that Francisca could have such influence over a great preacher such as Ortiz alarmed the Inquisition, and the Superior of the Franciscan monastery to which Ortiz belonged implored the Inquisitor-General to curtail the activities of this woman.

When Adrian of Utrecht had been elected Pope, Alfonso Manrique, the Cardinal and Archbishop of Seville, had been appointed Inquisitor-General in his place. Manrique was not so impressed by Francisca as Adrian had been, and he thought it would be a good plan if she was ordered to retire to a convent. He therefore suggested that she should be received into Santa Isabel; but the Superior of this convent was immediately alarmed at the thought of having such a disturbing element in her convent, and refused to receive Francisca.

Francisca however did leave Valladolid and, when she did so, Ortiz joined her at Castillo Tejeriego.

That he should have disobeyed the order of his superior was considered decidedly shocking and he was ordered to return to the monastery and never to see or have any communication with Francisca again.

Ortiz answered this command by declaring that Francisca was the beloved of God, and it was more important to obey the orders of God than even those of the Superior of his monastery.

The Inquisition was more concerned over Ortiz than over Francisca, because he was such a remarkable preacher and the Church had urgent need of such men. Therefore it was agreed that Francisca should be once more arrested, it being assumed that if she could be proved to be an impostor, Ortiz would cease to be her devoted admirer.

It was arranged that Francisca should be arrested after

Easter of the year 1529. Ortiz was expected to preach during Holy Week, and it was thought very necessary that he should not be disturbed at this time; for this reason it was decided to postpone the arrest.

News reached Ortiz of what was afoot and he visited Manrique imploring him to leave Francisca in peace. Manrique replied firmly that Ortiz himself had better take care, for his connection with Francisca brought him under suspicion; and it was solely due to the fact that he was such a popular preacher that he was being allowed his freedom.

Francisca was accordingly arrested after Easter and was put under guard, not in a prison but in a private house, so careful were the Inquisitors not to make a false step. But when Ortiz, hearing of her arrest, hurried to her, she was immediately removed to the secret prison of the Inquisition.

Ortiz then did a very foolish thing. He was so enamoured of Francisca that he thought of nothing but securing her immediate release through popular protest.

On 6th April he was to preach in the Franciscan Church and, as usual on those occasions when he graced the pulpit, the church was full to overflowing. He was certainly very brave, for he was fully aware of the power of the Inquisition. Obedience to God, he said, was more important than obedience to man. He did not pretend to be a prophet but he was certain that God would inflict great punishment on those who had committed the sin of arresting the beloved of God, Francisca Hernandez.

This was a direct insult and challenge to the Inquisitor-General and there was an immediate outcry against Ortiz, who was pulled down from the pulpit and hurried to a nearby house. There he was left some hours before he was taken to the prison of the Inquisition.

A wild fanaticism possessed Ortiz; he had criticized the dreaded Inquisition in public and he could not expect to escape its vengeance. He declared that he cared nothing for the Inquisition; he only cared for Francisca. He would found a new society for the honour of God and Truth, and if necessary this would work in opposition to the Holy Office. He would not retract a word of his sermon.

When he heard that he was accused of unbecoming love for Francisca he declared that she, being the bride of Christ, was as God himself and however much love he bore her could not be too much. He went on to say that it mattered not if one fasted or feasted, or how one lived, as long as there was love of God in one's life. He pointed out – a very dangerous thing to do – how the doctrines of the Church had changed from time to time and how what was considered right at one time was wrong at another.

There are no records of Francisca's trial, although her name is mentioned in connection with other trials; and it would appear from these that she was easily persuaded to give evidence against former friends.

As usual in the affairs of the Inquisition the formalities were many and the delays considerable; thus in 1532, Francisca was still a prisoner of the Inquisition, although by this time she was no longer in the *carceles secretas* but was living in a private house and was allowed to have a maid to wait on her.

It may have been that the Inquisition was loath to punish one who had a reputation for sanctity; or it may have been that they found her a useful witness against many people; but the fact remains that the Inquisition dealt leniently with Francisa.

And when one compares the treatment of Ortiz with that of *Marranos, Moriscos* and Lutherans one is amazed at the tolerance displayed in this instance by the Inquisition.

It must be remembered that Ortiz had actually dared criticize the Inquisitor-General, behaviour which would have meant certain death to any who was considered a heretic. Ortiz however was put in prison and whilst there Luis Coronel, a secretary of the Inquisitor-General, was sent to him to try to make him retract his recent statements.

He refused however and, being sure that he was possessed of the glory of God, he stoically endured imprisonment, not omitting during that time to undergo the privations of a man determined to live the spiritual life. He gave up eating meat, slept on a plank, and wore his hair shirt continually.

Ortiz had been too popular a man for the Inquisition to treat him like any common heretic. Even the Princess Juana asked for his release. This was when his brother Doctor Pedro Ortiz was to be sent to Rome on a royal commission, and it seemed to Juana that it was unfitting that the brother of a man who was engaged on such a mission should be a prisoner.

The commission undertaken by Doctor Pedro Ortiz was a very important one, for at this time Henry VIII, having become enamoured of Anne Boleyn, was seeking to prove that his marriage to Catalina of Aragon was no true marriage. As a result of this there was a great stir of activity in England, Spain and Rome.

But the Inquisitor-General could not allow insults to be hurled at him and the Holy Office and be ignored, and even the request of Princess Juana did not bring about the release of Ortiz.

Eventually after several years of imprisonment the influence of Francisca Hernandez seemed to weaken, and Ortiz was prepared to acknowledge his errors.

As a result he was sentenced to do penance for vehement suspicion of heresy. He walked in a procession, carrying a lighted taper, to the cathedral where he heard his sentence. For two more years he would remain in a cell, which he must not leave, in the convent of Torrelaguna; for five years he must not perform the functions of a priest; he must perform certain penances at regular intervals; he was not to communicate in any way whatsoever with Francisca Hernandez nor live within five miles of her.

If he disobeyed any of these rules he would at once be condemned to the stake, where he would meet the fate of a relapsed heretic.

The Inquisition believed that he could do great good for the Church if his mind were purged of all unorthodox ideas and heresies; and at the end of his sentence they wished him to resume his preaching.

However, Ortiz could not after all his years of imprisonment tear himself away from the life he had lived in his cell at Torrelaguna. There he became renowned for his sanctity; he apparently had no more desire to get into touch with Francisca;

all he wished for was to lead the life of a recluse. Perhaps his encounter with the Inquisition had taught him that it was the safest way.

However he remained at Torrelaguna until he died in the year 1546.

The Inquisition had certainly shown great leniency towards these two people.

Another interesting case is that of Magdalena de la Cruz who appeared on the scene some time before the famous Francisca Hernandez

Magdalena was born somewhere about 1487, at that time when the interest in mysticism was beginning to grow in Spain. It was small wonder that many aspiring young girls, seeing what happened to those who declared they were imbued with especial holiness, should wish to share in the triumph.

Magladena let it be believed that when she was four years old she had her first vision of the Virgin, who gave her a detailed account of the life and death of Christ. Precocious Magdalena immediately believed that she would like to follow in the Master's footsteps and, since there was no one at hand ready to crucify her, she decided to perform the act herself. Before however she got so far as nailing herself to the cross she fell and broke her ribs. Although she had failed in this attempt, for one so young to have made it was considered to be a sign of future holiness.

Magdalena told many stories about her childhood adventures – how once she had run away from home and was suddenly carried through the air back to her bedroom; how she had once heard that the Sacrament was being taken to a dying man and, wishing to see it pass her father's house, she had been unable to do so because there was no window in her room. Suddenly, and miraculously, she discovered a crack in the wall and through this she saw the Sacrament. It was said that whenever the Sacrament passed a house in which was Magdalena, the wall opened that she might see it pass.

She was clearly a hysterical and precocious little girl who was absolutely certain what she intended to do in life. She was going to be a *Beata*; and she set about acquiring a reputation for sanctity.

When she was seventeen she went into the Convent of Santa Isobel de los Angeles at Cordova. There she delighted her fellow nuns with her trances and miracles. She declared that there was a spirit who was constantly at her side.

She was an adept at producing miracles; she was of such a hysterical nature that she was able to produce certain physical reactions which were the delight of her fellow nuns.

There is a story that she wished to experience all that the Virgin Mary had experienced in giving birth to Christ, and that she told the nuns that her spiritual guardian had promised her that she should do this.

Strangely enough her body began to swell and on Christmas Day she was found seated in her cell holding what appeared to be a baby in her arms. The child was hidden by the hair which hung from her head but which was not really her own hair – presumably a wig she had acquired to guard the child from too curious eyes.

It must have been very exciting to have such a person in the convent, for there were no dull moments with Magdalena around.

That she should develop that commonplace manifestation of holiness, the stigmata, was inevitable.

Her reputation of course grew, and the most miraculous happenings were accredited to her. The sick believed that a touch from her was enough to cure them; sailors prayed to her to intercede for them when storms beset them; ladies who were about to bear children asked her blessings. Before the birth of Philip II, his mother, the Empress Isabella sent his layette to the convent that Magdalena might bless it. Even the Pope asked Magdalena to use her special influence with the Deity for the sake of the Church.

Magdalena was at the height of her power. She became Prioress of the convent; this was very good for the convent, as gifts of great magnificence were constantly being showered on the holy woman, and Magdalena took nothing for herself but gave everything to the convent.

A rumour went round that she lived on nothing but the Eucharist. One of those who doubted her very extraordinary stories suggested that since she lived without food she would have no hesitation in allowing herself to be shut up in a cell where none could reach her, and thus prove that she could exist without food and drink.

Magdalena stayed for two days and nights in this cell, and when she was nearly exhausted she managed to escape – no doubt with the help of some of the nuns. She declared then that St Francis and St Anthony had come to her aid and had removed her from the cell.

So this attempt to prove her a fraud merely rebounded to her credit.

But Magdalena was unlucky. In the year 1543, nearly forty years after she had first entered the convent, she became very ill. So sick was she that her physicians were sure she could not live, and she was warned to prepare for the end.

She then confessed that she had deceived them all, that her miracles had been fakes and that she had been possessed not by holy spirits but by evil ones. She begged forgiveness for her sins.

It was very unfortunate for Magdalena, because she did not die; and when she recovered there was only one thing to be done; the Inquisition must step in.

Magdalena was certainly a hysterical woman; she undoubtedly believed that she had been possessed. She told the Inquisitors that a demon had taken possession of her when she was a child. She admitted that she had invented many of the miracles and had used her skill to delude people into accepting them as truth.

She was condemned to appear at an *auto* in the Cathedral of Cordova and there recount her sins in detail; she was forced to stand on the scaffold, a gag in her mouth, a lighted taper in her hand and a rope round her neck, while she listened to her sentence.

Once again the Inquisition was lenient. Her sentence was that she must live in perpetual retirement and each day for a year she must perform her penance; she was not to receive the sacrament for three years.

Thus Magdalena outlived her glory; she then began to live a life of spirituality and, by 1560 when she died, she had lived for several years in quiet seclusion, serene, dutiful to the laws of the convent – in fact the hysterical self-advertising woman had become a model of humility.

The effect of a case such as that of Magdalena de la Cruz was to deter other women from following a like course. Quite understandably, while all Spain was talking of the way in which Magdalena had deceived thousands, they were unlikely to be duped by the extraordinary adventures of some other bright girl.

Maria de la Visitacion was Portuguese; but Portugal was at this time under the control of Philip II.

She was eleven when she went into the convent of La Anunziata in Lisbon. By the time she was sixteen she was having visions of Christ, and so convincing was she that by the time she was twenty-seven she was made Prioress of the convent.

News of her fame spread through Portugal and Spain and was even carried to Rome.

It was said that when she was praying she would often be lifted from her knees and appear to float upwards. She also declared that she had a vision of Christ suffering on the cross; fire came from his side and touched hers. There was a mark on her side to prove this, and on Fridays it bled, giving her a great deal of pain. On her hands the stigmata appeared in the form of nail holes, and each Thursday she suffered from a pain in the head which she said was like a crown of thorns pressing into her skin. Then it was discovered that her brow was punctured as though by thorns and from these punctures blood flowed.

It was her habit to place pieces of cloth against the wound in her side and these became marked with spots of blood – five of them arranged in the form of a cross. Naturally these pieces of linen were considered relics of the utmost holiness. Even the Pope received one.

Maria however was not content with being merely a holy woman. So much adulation came her way that she wished to play a bigger role in her country's affairs.

Portugal was restive under the rule of Philip, and when certain Portuguese decided to revolt against the Spanish yoke they sought the advice of Maria. Maria immediately became an ardent supporter of the plot, which was eventually betrayed.

Since she had dabbled in politics she had become a woman of political importance who could not be ignored, and the Inquisition was anxious to prove her an impostor, for only thus could they rob her of her influence and power.

A deputation visited her convent, but before seeing Maria they interviewed several of the nuns; it did not take the subtle Inquisitors long to draw what they wanted from the frightened women, who were ready to admit that Maria had been playing certain tricks on those who were foolish enough to be duped by them.

Then Maria was sent for. She was warned that she must tell the truth. She persisted that she had always told the truth and that any who had spoken against her had lied.

The Inquisitors declared their desire to see the stigmata, and when it was shown to them they pinioned Maria, sent for hot water and with vigorous application were able to wash away the painted marks.

When Maria saw that she was exposed she fell sobbing at the feet of the Inquisitors, begged for mercy, and told them that she would make a full confession.

She explained that she had painted the stigmata on her hands; the wounds in her side and on her forehead had been self-inflicted; the blood-stained linen was carefully prepared before it was pressed to her side and produced by sleight of hand; she was evidently something of a conjuror, and she had many tricks at her finger-tips.

She was more harshly sentenced than Magdalena de la Cruz had been and was condemned to perpetual imprisonment in a Dominican convent. Every Wednesday and Friday she was to be whipped during the chanting of a Miserere; on Wednesdays and Fridays she was to have nothing but bread and water; every time she entered the refectory she was to repeat her crimes to the nuns, and she was to take her meals on the floor and afterwards lie across the doorway so that when the nuns

184

went out they could walk over her body. She was not to speak to anybody without first obtaining permission.

So Maria de la Visitacion passed the rest of her days and as she was only thirty-two years old when she was sentenced her punishment was a severe one. We are told that she accepted it with stoicism and grew truly pious.

The Inquisition was certainly more severe with Maria than with others of her kind, which leads to the conclusion that her case was meant to be a dire warning to any would-be holy women who sought to interfere in politics.

The case of Doña Teresa de Silva is another which throws light on the methods of the Inquisition.

When Teresa was twenty-two her confessor and spiritual guardian was Fray Francisco García Calderón. Teresa had been an invalid for some years and was clearly an hysterical person. She was one of those girls who wished to call attention to herself by the difference between her life and that of others around her; and the only way to do this was to stress her spirituality. It was not long before miracles were being attributed to her.

She entered a Benedictine Order and was elected Abbess. Calderón was made confessor or spiritual father of the convent.

The situation in which a man was a frequent visitor to a convent had its effect on the women enclosed therein – rather naturally many were hysterical types, and the first sign that all was not well occurred when one of the nuns began throwing the images about. A doctor was sent for. He declared that she was not insane but possessed by a devil. Calderón then set about the task of exorcism but without success. The nun remained 'possessed' and, after watching her unaccountable behaviour, two other nuns began to imitate her.

Teresa was horrified, and to her dismay she found herself becoming hysterical in exactly the same way as the nuns. Calderón sought to exorcise her, but his efforts were in vain; and the sickness, or whatever it was, began to spread through the convent until all the nuns – except five – were acting in this

185

most extraordinary manner, throwing themselves as well as the sacred images about the convent and uttering such obscenities that all were sure that wicked devils were in possession of their bodies, for the nuns could not possibly understand the words they uttered.

This state of affairs persisted for three years and gradually scandal began to attach itself to the convent. There was something basically wrong, people said; and this was an outward manifestation of that wrongness. Was this connected with Calderón's presence in the convent? It was strange that a man should be allowed to make so free with nuns – and he a priest.

A one-time friend of Calderón (but a friend no longer) named Fray Alonso de Leon thought it was high time the Inquisition took a hand; and he reported the strange manifestations at the convent to his Inquisitor and expressed his belief that some heresy was being committed to produce such a result.

Calderón, being warned that the Inquisition was about to make an investigation, decided to leave hastily for France. This he attempted, but he was seized by the *alguazils* before he could make good his escape.

Teresa and her nuns were taken from their convent and brought to the *carceles secretas* at Toledo.

Calderón was brought before the tribunal. He would admit to no wrong-doing. He was then taken to the torture chambers, first shown the dreaded instruments, then stripped and finally submitted to the most extreme torture. He was a brave man. He assured the Inquisitors that there had been no wrong-doing at the convent; the nuns had been truly possessed by demons.

The hysterical nuns however lacked his calm; placed in solitude and never allowed to forget the threat of torture, they were ready to say what was required of them.

Thus on the 27th of April, 1630, an *auto particular* took place in the hall of the Holy House at Toledo.

Calderón was brought forward and a list of his sins was read to him. He was charged with being an *Alumbrado*. It was recalled against him that years before he had lived in an immoral relationship with a young girl whom he had caused to be

186

treated as a *beata*, and whom when she died he had buried as though she were a saint, leaving a place for his own grave beside her, and trying to make the world believe that she had performed many miracles. He had declared that to suffer from demoniac possession was a sign of God's approval; he was also accused of trying to reform the Church and planning to make himself Pope. Other charges were brought against him, such as trying to persuade a young woman that if she would submit to him he could give her a child who would one day be Pope.

Even under the cruellest torture he had refused to admit to these crimes, and this, in the eyes of the Inquisition, increased his guilt.

His punishment was to be taken to Valladolid where he should go to a convent of his Order, and there his crimes would be enumerated while a circular whipping took place; which meant that all the monks present surrounded him and delivered blows; then he was to be taken to another convent where he would again suffer the circular beating. He was to be imprisoned for life in a cell and never allowed to perform the functions of a priest; he must fast three days every week and only be allowed to receive the Sacrament at Christmas, Easter and Pentecost.

As for Doña Teresa, she was sent to another convent for four years; the nuns were to be separated and sent to different convents.

Seven years later Teresa appealed against her sentence, and the Supreme Council of the Inquisition agreed to reconsider it. Teresa won her case. She was released from her sentence, as were all the nuns.

No one seemed in the least anxious about poor Calderón. Perhaps by this time he had died of shame, loneliness, fasting and circular scourging.

The methods of the Inquisition grew more severe against mystics as time passed. Torture was freely used to extort confessions, but this did not prevent *beatas* appearing in large numbers.

Thousands of women developed the stigmata on their hands,

so that this phenomenon ceased to excite a great deal of attention. Men and women, wishing for the prestige which came from holiness, were not always ready to live the life of privation to achieve this. New doctrines appeared. There was the case of Juan de Jesus who declared himself unaware of carnal desires; he only knew the demands of his spirit. Thus he was able to indulge those desires for he insisted that they were quite unimportant, and whether indulged or not it did not matter. He even went so far as to announce that he had had a revelation in which he had been shown that all women who gave themselves – and alms – to him would be certain of salvation.

The Inquisition eventually caught him. He was not punished with real severity. He was given a hundred lashes and confined for the rest of his days to a convent where he was to work hard for his bread.

There is no doubt that many of these men and women believed – or half-believed – the fantastic stories they caused to be circulated about themselves. Today they would be given psychiatric treatment; and because they would not be in an enviable position few would wish to emulate them and work themselves up into a fervour of hysteria until they reached this state of half-belief. But what a temptation it was in sixteenth-, seventeenth-, eighteenth- and nineteenth-century Spain. Any obscure little girl could call attention to herself, could receive – if only temporarily – the adulation of the multitude, by painting the stigmata on her hands or even wounding herself with a sharp knife. The slight inconvenience must have seemed well worth while since as a result she was lifted from boredom and obscurity to fame and adulation.

Cases of mystics are recorded from the early fifteenth century to the very end of the Inquisition in the nineteenth. The case of Maria de los Dolores López gives an indication as to how the Inquisition had changed during three centuries. The trial of Beata Dolores took place in 1779; and at this time the Inquisition was growing near to its twilight hour.

Beata Dolores had left home at the age of twelve to live in the house of her confessor. Precocious and sensuous she quickly became the Confessor's mistress.

Dolores was full of wiles. She pretended that she was blind, and the fact that she could read, write and do exquisite embroidery was considered a miracle.

When the Confessor who had been her lover died, Dolores was well equipped to look after herself. Thousands flocked to see the blind woman who was aware of what went on about her as though she could see. She held long conversations with her guardian angel; and this way of life proved very profitable for those who visited her brought gifts of great value; and her fame spread.

She could not however live long without masculine companionship and took another confessor. This man very quickly realized that he was to fill a double role – that of confessor and lover.

Dolores must have been a very attractive woman and the confessor, having recovered from his first shock of surprise, succumbed.

Unfortunately for Dolores, this man was possessed of a conscience, and to relieve this he went before the tribunal of Seville and confessed their relationship.

As a result the confessor was sent to a convent where he was to live in rigid seclusion. Beata Dolores was brought before the tribunal.

She assured the Inquisitors that, since she was four years old, she had been in communication with the Virgin Mary and had been married to Christ in Heaven.

She would have been given some light sentence had she not insisted on defending her sensuality with the doctrine called Molinist after Miguel de Molinos. The theme of this was that what appeared to be evil to ordinary mortals was not so if condoned by God. She maintained that the relationship which she had enjoyed with her men friends had in no way offended Christ and the Virgin and therefore was not evil. This was, of course, in direct contrast to the teaching of the Church and could only come under the heading of heresy.

Dolores however refused to accept the Church's view and clung to her own, so giving the Inquisition no alternative but to brand her as a heretic. There was only one penalty for such heresy: burning at the stake.

However, with the Inquisition in twilight at this time, 1781, burnings were not so frequent nor so popular as they had once been, and efforts were made to make Dolores turn from her heresy and be received into the Church.

Dolores was a strange woman. She must have believed in herself, for knowing that a fiery death awaited her, she refused as stubbornly as had the earlier martyrs.

There was no help for it; she was conducted to the *auto de fé*; and it was necessary to put a gag in her mouth, for she insisted on shouting her dangerous views to the crowd. But the sight of the faggots ready to be kindled broke her spirit as no amount of talking could do. Dolores broke down, confessed, and was strangled before the wood at her feet was set alight.

Thus in its treatment of mystics, the Spanish Inquisition appears to have behaved with admirable restraint and even mercy, although, naturally, in these more enlightened days, floggings and solitary confinement seem harsh enough punishment to be meted out to those who are suffering from unbalanced minds. There is no doubt that many of the so-called mystics were clever impostors and these too were treated with a leniency which was amazing considering the times.

It was upon the Jews, Moors and Lutherans that the Inquisitors vented their demoniacal fury; and in the sixteenth century when fanatical Philip was desirous of setting it up in every country over which he had control, the growth of the Spanish Inquisition continued and reached its hideous heyday.

PRINCIPAL WORKS CONSULTED

Acton, John Emerich Edward Dalberg, First Baron Acton, D.C.L., LL.D. Edited with an introduction by John Neville Figgis, M.A., and Reginald Vere Laurence, M.A. *The History of Freedom and Other Essays.* (1907)

Adams, Nicholson B. *The Heritage of Spain: An Introduction to Spanish Civilization.* (1949)

Alberti, L. de, and Chapman, A. B. Wallis, D.Sc. (Econ.), Edited by. *English Merchants and the Spanish Inquisition in the Canaries.* Extracts from the Archives in possession of the Most Hon. The Marquess of Bute. (1912)

Aradi, Zsolt. *The Popes.* (1956)

Aubrey, William Hickman Smith. *History of England.*

Bainton, Roland H. *The Reformation of the 16th Century.* (1953)

Bainton, Roland H. *The Travail of Religious Liberty.* (1953)

Baker, The Rev. J., M.A. *The History of the Inquisition as it subsists in the Kingdoms of Spain, Portugal, etc., and in both the Indies to this day.* (1734)

Berdyaev, Nicholas. With a Commentary and Notes by Alan A. Spears. Translated by Alan A. Spears and Victor B. Kanter. *Christianity and Anti-Semitism.* (1952)

Bertrand, Louis of the Académie Française and Sir Charles Petrie, Bt., M.A., F.R.Hist.S. *The History of Spain.* (1934)

Bury, J. B. With an Epilogue by Blackham, H. J. *A History of Freedom of Thought.* (1952)

Butterfield, Herbert. *Christianity in European History.* (1951)

Cary-Elwes, Columbia, Monk of Ampleforth. With a Preface by Professor Arnold Toynbee. *Law, Liberty and Love.* (1949)

Creighton, M., D.D. *Persecution and Tolerance.* (1895)

Dawson, Christopher. *Religion and the Rise of Western Culture.* (1950)

Deanesly, M., M.A. *A History of the Medieval Church 590–1500.* (1925)

Giffard, William Ava. *The Story of the Faith.* A Survey of Christian History for the Undogmatic. (1946)

Gordon, Janet. *The Spanish Inquisition: Its Heroes and Martyrs.* (1898)

Gowen, Herbert H., D.D., F.R.A.S. *A History of Religion.* (1934)

Guizot, M. Translated by Robert Black, M.A. *The History of France from Earliest Times to the Year 1789.* (1881)

Hope, Thomas. *Torquemada, Scourge of the Jews.* (1939)

Hume, Martin A. S. Revised by Edward Armstrong. *Spain, Its Greatness and Decay* (1479–1788). Cambridge Historical Series. (1931)

Lea, Henry Charles, LL.D. *A History of the Inquisition of the Middle Ages.* 3 Volumes. (1901)

Lea, Henry Charles, LL.D. *A History of the Inquisition of Spain.* 4 Volumes. (1907)

Lea, Henry Charles, LL.D. *Superstition and Force.* (1892)

Lea, Henry Charles, LL.D. *The Inquisition in the Spanish Dependencies.* (1908)

Limborch, Philip. *The History of the Inquisition as it has Subsisted in France, Italy, Spain, Portugal, Venice, Sicily, Sardinia, Milan, Poland, Flanders, etc.* (1816)

Marchant, John, and others. *A Review of the Bloody Tribunal*; or the *Horrid Cruelties of the Inquisition, as practised in Spain, Portugal, Italy, and the East and West Indies, on all those whom the Church of Rome brands with the name of Hereticks.* (1770)

Maycock, A. L., M.A. With an Introduction by Father Ronald Knox. *The Inquisition from its Establishment to the Great Schism.* (1926)

McKinnon, James, PhD., D.D., D.Th., LL.D. *Calvin and the Reformation.* (1936)

McKnight, John P. *The Papacy.* (1953)

Merton, Reginald. *Cardinal Ximenes and the Making of Spain.* (1934)

Mortimer, R.C., M.A., B.D. *The Elements of Moral Theology.* (1947)

Nickerson, Hoffman. With a Preface by Hilaire Belloc. *The Inquisition. A Political and Military Study of its Establishment.* (1923)

Poole, Reginald Lane. *Illustrations of the History of Medieval Thought and Learning.* (1880)

Prescott, William H. *History of the Reign of Ferdinand and Isabella the Catholic.* 2 Volumes.

Prescott, William H. *History of the Reign of Philip II, King of Spain.* 3 Volumes. (1879)

Robertson, John M. *A Short History of Freethought, Ancient and Modern.* 2 Volumes. (1915)

Roth, Cecil. *The Spanish Inquisition.* (1937)

Rule, William Harris, D.D. *A History of the Inquisition.* 2 Volumes. (1874)

Sabatini, Rafael. *Torquemada and the Spanish Inquisition.* (1928)

Shewring, Walter (Translated and Introduced by). *Rich and Poor in Christian Tradition.* Writings of many centuries. (1947)

Simon, Dr Paul. Translated from the German by Meyrick Booth, Ph.D. *The Human Element in the Church of Christ.* (1953)

Stephen, James Fitzjames, Q.C. *Liberty, Equality, Fraternity.* (1873)

Swain, John. *The Pleasures of the Torture Chamber.* (1931)

Turberville, A. S., M.C, M.A., B.Litt. *Medieval Heresy and the Inquisition.* (1920)

Turberville, A. S., M.C., M.A., B.Litt. *The Spanish Inquisition.* (1932)

Wiseman, F., M.A. *Roman Spain. An Introduction to the Antiquities of Spain and Portugal.* (1956)

The Catholic Encyclopedia: An International Work of Reference on the Constitution, Doctrine, Discipline and History of the Catholic Church. Edited by Charles G. Herbermann, Ph.D., LL.D., Edward A. Pace, Ph.D., D.D, Condé B. Pallen, Ph.D., L.L.D., Thomas J. Shahan, D.D., John J. Wynne, SJ, assisted by numerous collaborators. (1907)

INDEX

0352   Star

301392	Linda Blandford **OIL SHEIKHS**	95p
396121	Anthony Cave Brown **BODYGUARD OF LIES** (Large Format)	£1.95*
301368	John Dean **BLIND AMBITION**	£1.00*
300124	Dr. F. Dodson **HOW TO PARENT**	75p*·
301457	**THE FAMILY DICTIONARY OF SYMPTOMS**	95p*
398914	J. Paul Getty **HOW TO BE RICH**	60p*
397829	**HOW TO BE A SUCCESSFUL EXECUTIVE**	60p*
398566	Harry Lorayne & Jerry Lucas **THE MEMORY BOOK**	60p*
39692X	Henry Miller **THE WORLD OF SEX**	60p
395311	Neville Randall & Gary Keane **FOCUS ON FACT:** **THE WORLD OF INVENTION** (illus)	75p
39532X	**THE STORY OF SPORT** (illus)	75p
39529X	**THE PSYCHIC WORLD** (illus)	75p
395303	**THE STORY OF CHRISTMAS** (illus)	75p
395338	**UNSOLVED MYSTERIES** (illus)	75p
397640	David Reuben **HOW TO GET MORE OUT OF SEX**	85p*
398779	Fiona Richmond **FIONA**	50p
396040	Idries Shah **THE SUFIS** (Large Format)	£1.95
395478	Michael Smith **THE DUCHESS OF DUKE STREET** **ENTERTAINS**	£1.50 ◆

Wyndham Books are obtainable from many booksellers and newsagents. If you have any difficulty please send purchase price plus postage on the scale below to:

Wyndham Cash Sales,
PO Box 11,
Falmouth,
Cornwall.

OR

Star Book Service,
G.P.O. Box 29,
Douglas,
Isle of Man,
British Isles.

While every effort is made to keep prices low, it is sometimes necessary to increase prices at short notice. Wyndham Books reserve the right to show new retail prices on covers which may differ from those advertised in the text or elsewhere.

Postage and Packing Rate
U.K.
One book 22p plus 10p per copy for each additional book ordered to a maximum charge of 82p.

B.F.P.O. & Eire
One book 22p plus 10p per copy for the next 6 books, and thereafter 4p per book.

Overseas
One book 30p plus 10p per copy for each additional book.

These charges are subject to Post Office charge fluctuations